Deception
Incidences whr
reality mathurs.

- Witches, supernatural (dagger)
- Burning wood to conceal bad
- Cover-up of murder    news

Equivocation (what the witches do) not telling
the whole
- Witches represent Macbeth's     truth.
  ~~power~~ ambition.
- Irony is small example of equivocation
- Duncan: plays with people. Not sure of
  his intention.
- Porter: comedy
    figure

Supernatural: Ghosts,
dagger, witches, apparitions
sleepwalking,    come from the
weather changes with devil.
the witches.

Fate: predictions → witches

Fertility & children: Banquo has lineage,
Macbeth is going to hell for killing the king
His children are slaughtered.
Malcolm becomes the future.
Macbeth meets the witches in an unfertile place
to represent fertility.

# Macbeth

SERIES EDITOR:
**JOHN SEELY**

EDITORIAL MATERIAL and ACTIVITIES:
**JOHN SEELY**
**RICHARD DURANT**
**FRANK GREEN**
**ELIZABETH SEELY**

Part of Pearson

Heinemann is an imprint of Pearson Education Limited, a company incorporated in
England and Wales, having its registered office at Edinburgh Gate, Harlow, Essex,
CM20 2JE. Registered company number: 872828

www.pearsonschoolsandfecolleges.co.uk

Heinemann is a registered trademark of Pearson Education Limited

Editorial material and activities © John Seely Partnership, Richard Durant and
Frank Green
All other material © Pearson Education Limited 2010

The right of John Seely Partnership, Richard Durant and Frank Green to be
identified as the authors of this work has been asserted by them in accordance with
the Copyright, Designs and Patents Act 1988.

First published 1994
This new edition published 2010

12 11
10 9 8 7 6 5 4 3

**British Library Cataloguing in Publication Data**
A catalogue record for this book is available from the British Library

ISBN 9780435026448

Typeset by Redmoor Design, Tavistock, Devon
Original illustrations © Pearson Education Limited, 2005
Illustrated by Roger Wade Walker
Cover photo © Photostage Ltd
Printed and bound in China (CTPS/03)

Every effort has been made to contact copyright holders of material reproduced in
this book. Any omissions will be rectified in subsequent printings if notice is given
to the publishers.

# CONTENTS

# The story of the play

## Act 1

### Scene 1

Three witches meet during a storm and plan to meet a man named Macbeth. They have links with the spirit world.

### Scene 2

King Duncan, his sons Malcolm and Donalbain, and Lennox receive news of a battle from a wounded captain. The rebellion of the Highlanders and Islanders has been defeated. Macbeth, the Thane of Glamis, has played an important part in the victory. But as soon as the battle was over, Sweno, King of Norway, attacked the tired soldiers with his fresh troops. Again, Macbeth's great bravery won the day. The Thane of Ross now hurries in to report the treachery of the Thane of Cawdor, who had always been close to Duncan. But seeing his advantage, Cawdor went over to the Norwegian side. They lost. Duncan instantly condemns Cawdor to death and names Macbeth new Thane of Cawdor.

### Scene 3

Macbeth and his friend Banquo meet the witches, apparently by chance. Macbeth is greeted by his correct title and also as Thane of Cawdor. Then the third witch says he will become king. Macbeth is startled; both men are amazed. Banquo asks about his own future. He is told that he will never become king, but his descendants will be kings. The witches disappear. Macbeth and Banquo wonder if they are going mad.

Ross and Angus, another lord, greet them and give Macbeth the title the witches have predicted: Thane of Cawdor. Macbeth asks Banquo whether he feels more confident that his children will be kings. Banquo tries to warn him that they may yet be harmed by the witches' predictions. He has seen Macbeth's temptation. The idea of murder begins to enter Macbeth's thoughts.

### Scene 4

The treacherous Thane of Cawdor has been executed. Duncan praises Macbeth in person. He promises honours and favours to him and to Banquo. Immediately afterwards Duncan names his son Malcolm as

Prince of Cumberland, the first step to his becoming crowned king on Duncan's death. This is a hard blow to Macbeth's hopes, but not the end of them. The king now announces he is coming to stay at the Macbeths' castle in Inverness and Macbeth leaves to alert his wife.

## Scene 5

Lady Macbeth has received a letter from her husband telling her about the witches. She reads it out, but comments to herself that she doubts her husband could ever be ruthless enough to go 'the shortest route' to kingship. This would mean the murder of Duncan. When she learns that Duncan is to be her guest overnight she starts to plan ways and means.

## Scene 6

Banquo and Duncan arrive at the castle. It is a pleasant evening. Duncan pays compliments to his hostess.

## Scene 7

Macbeth broods about the planned murder. It is only ambition that drives him to it. He tells Lady Macbeth he has decided not to do it. She is determined and has a plan. Duncan will be killed in his sleep. It will look as though his guards have done it. Macbeth agrees to the plan.

# Act 2

## Scene 1

Late at night, Macbeth comes across Banquo and his son Fleance. They agree to discuss their experience with the witches when they have time. When Macbeth is alone he seems to see a dagger leading him on. He cannot take hold of it and realises that it is an hallucination. Suddenly the dagger drips with blood. A bell rings – Lady Macbeth is giving him the signal to go and kill Duncan.

## Scene 2

The guards have been drugged and their daggers have been laid ready by Lady Macbeth. Macbeth returns, having done the deed. His hands are covered in blood. He is upset by what he has done. His wife tells him to go and wash and replace the grooms' daggers, which he has foolishly brought away with him. He cannot go back, so she does. Suddenly there is a knocking at the gate. Lady Macbeth says they must wash and make it appear that they have been in bed.

## Scene 3

The drunken porter at the gate talks fantastically about being the porter for Hell. He lets in Macduff and Lennox. Macbeth greets them. Macduff goes to wake the king. A moment later he returns from Duncan's room having seen the murdered king. They are all horrified. It seems that the grooms are to blame. Macbeth admits that he has killed them in his fury. As he speaks, Lady Macbeth faints and is carried out. Duncan's sons are worried for their own safety and leave without meeting up with the others. Malcolm goes to England and Donalbain to Ireland.

## Scene 4

An old man chats to Ross about the weird happenings. The disappearance of the king's sons makes it look as though they are guilty of the murder. Macbeth is about to be crowned king. Duncan's body has been taken to lie with his ancestors. Macduff goes home instead of attending Macbeth's coronation.

# Act 3

## Scene 1

Banquo feels sure that Macbeth is responsible for Duncan's death. Macbeth and his queen greet Banquo as the most important guest for their banquet. He and his son have planned to ride before dinner. Macbeth sees them off and then talks to two murderers. He persuades the two men that their misfortunes are Banquo's fault, then says he will give them instructions on how to carry out the deed.

## Scene 2

Macbeth and his wife separately regret the state they are in. They would be more at peace dead than having terrible dreams. However they must play the part of gracious king and queen at the banquet.

## Scene 3

The murderers attack Banquo and his son. Banquo is killed but Fleance escapes.

## Scene 4

The feast is set up and the lords take their places. One of the murderers tells Macbeth that Banquo is dead but his son has escaped. Macbeth returns to the table but cannot find an empty seat –

Banquo's ghost has taken his. Macbeth is completely unnerved at the sight and accuses the lords of playing a trick on him. Lady Macbeth has to invent a history of these sudden 'fits'. After a while she has to bring dinner to an end. Macduff is suspect because he has not attended.

## Scene 5

The three witches are scolded by their queen, Hecate. They have acted without her permission. She has nasty plans for Macbeth.

## Scene 6

Lennox makes it plain to another lord that he doesn't believe the official story about who killed Duncan. The lord says that Malcolm and Macduff have fled to England to ask for help.

# Act 4

## Scene 1

The three witches meet again to wait for Macbeth and are preparing a magic potion. They show Macbeth three apparitions. He is told to beware of Macduff, but also that 'none of woman born' can harm him, and that he cannot be overcome until Birnam Wood moves up to Dunsinane Hill. Macbeth accepts all this but he also wants to know about Banquo's heirs. He is shown a line of eight kings. The witches disappear. Lennox arrives and tells Macbeth that Macduff has fled to England. Macbeth decides that Macduff's family must be killed.

## Scene 2

In Macduff's castle his wife cannot understand why her husband has abandoned her and her children. A messenger warns her to escape, but the murderers arrive, kill her son and pursue his mother.

## Scene 3

In the English king's palace, Malcolm tests Macduff's loyalty and honour, saying he is even more wicked than Macbeth, but without any of the qualities which make a good king. Macduff's response to each of these untrue statements convinces Malcolm to trust him. They will work and fight together for a better Scotland. There is a large English army already on the move. Ross arrives with the news of the slaughter of Macduff's family and servants. Macduff grieves but the news strengthens his resolve to kill Macbeth personally.

# Act 5

## Scene 1

At Inverness a doctor has been called to consider what is wrong with Lady Macbeth. She sleepwalks at night, appearing to try and wash blood from her hands. She speaks brokenly of what is troubling her. It doesn't make sense to her hearers, but what is plain is that she is very distressed and sick. The doctor does not know how to treat this.

## Scene 2

The English army approaches Macbeth's fortress at Dunsinane. People say Macbeth is mad. He is losing support. His remaining people just obey orders.

## Scene 3

Macbeth encourages himself by repeating the apparitions' predictions. News comes of the approaching English army. Macbeth insists he will fight and demands to have his armour. He asks after his wife but the doctor says he cannot cure her. Macbeth is disgusted with this response.

## Scene 4

At Birnam Wood, Malcolm orders the soldiers to cut down branches and use them as camouflage.

## Scene 5

Macbeth is preparing for a long siege. Lady Macbeth dies. Macbeth speaks of the brevity and insignificance of life. A messenger arrives claiming that he has seen Birnam Wood begin to move. Macbeth swears that he will die in armour.

## Scene 6

Malcolm orders the camouflage to be thrown down. Siward and his son will lead the first attack.

## Scene 7

In the battle, Macbeth fights Young Siward and kills him. Macduff sets out to find Macbeth. Macbeth's army begin to desert.

## Scene 8

Macduff and Macbeth meet and fight. Macbeth believes he cannot be beaten, until Macduff tells him he was born early by a Caesarean operation. They fight and Macduff kills Macbeth.

## Scene 9

Macduff enters with the severed head of Macbeth and hails Malcolm as king, who declares that the thanes shall now become earls. Exiles from the terror will be recalled to Scotland and welcomed. They believe that Lady Macbeth committed suicide. Malcolm invites everyone to his crowning at Scone.

# Background to the play

## The source of *Macbeth*

Shakespeare often found the ideas for his plays in historical sources. The lives of great rulers with their dramatic conflicts provided excellent plots for plays. Shakespeare did not follow his sources closely, however. Instead, he took all the most interesting parts and sometimes added new material to make his plays exciting on the stage.

## The succession

The diagram below shows how the historical Macbeth became king after Duncan's death. As you can see, Macbeth and Duncan were cousins.

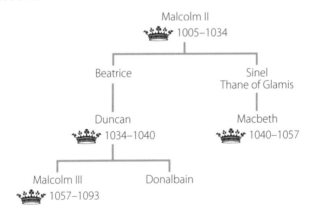

## Where Shakespeare found his information

Shakespeare used Holinshed's *Chronicles of England, Scotland and Ireland* as his source for *Macbeth*. In turn, Holinshed had based his work on earlier sources. However, Shakespeare has made a number of alterations and additions to Holinshed. One major change is that the play covers a period of a few months, whereas the real Macbeth ruled Scotland for 17 years; another is that in reality Macbeth was a good king and Duncan was weak, but in the play Macbeth is a tyrant and Duncan is highly respected.

There are some other changes too. In Holinshed's book:

- Lady Macbeth is mentioned only once
- the rebellion and invasion take place at different times
- Macdonald commits suicide
- Duncan is killed by hired assassins
- the drugging of guards and their murder is from a different period of Scottish history
- Banquo is involved in the death of Duncan
- Banquo is murdered after Macbeth's banquet, not before
- Macbeth flees from Macduff.

## Jacobean background

In 1603, Shakespeare's company of actors came under the patronage of James I, and they were known as the King's Men. *Macbeth* was probably first performed at court in August 1606 to mark the visit of James's brother-in-law, King Christian of Denmark.

Out of respect for his royal audience, Shakespeare made certain omissions from the historical story:

- Banquo knows nothing of the plot to kill Duncan
- no mention is made of the Danes who reinforced Sweno's army.

On the other hand, it is not surprising that on such an occasion Shakespeare included elements of which James I would approve:

- the qualities of good kingship (James had written a treatise on the art of government)
- the divine nature of kings
- the healing powers of kings
- James's family tree, including Banquo and Edward the Confessor (King of England in the play)
- the supernatural.

## Witchcraft

During the reign of Queen Elizabeth I (1533–1603) the public was increasingly preoccupied with witchcraft. In 1564, a law came into force making murder by witchcraft punishable by death, thus acknowledging witches and their supernatural powers. It is estimated that in Scotland alone 8,000 'witches' were burned to death between 1564 and 1603.

In 1604 an additional law was passed in Scotland, which declared that anyone found guilty of practising witchcraft should be executed. James I himself became personally involved with witchcraft when he and his wife, Anne, were almost shipwrecked on their return to Scotland from Denmark in 1590. In a notable case, a Dr Fian and the 'witches of Berwick' were found guilty of trying to kill the king and queen by raising storms at sea.

James I published a work on witchcraft, *Demonology*, in 1597. Although some people rebelled against this persecution, the belief in witches was widespread and the execution of witches did not cease until the end of the seventeenth century.

## Divine order

Jacobeans believed that the whole universe had an order to it that was decided by God. Anything unnatural was against this divine order. Kings were considered God's agents, so action against a king was a crime against God. They believed Satan had rebelled against God directly, and he was responsible, through witches and evil spirits, for all attacks on the divine order.

# The play

Although it is set in Scotland in 1040, *Macbeth* deals with issues that are relevant to any society in any age. It explores the far-reaching effects of one man's ambition, from the total transformation of that man's character to the nation-wide terror he provokes. At the beginning of the play Macbeth is co-leader of the Scottish army and a national hero. He increases his reputation with further victories, but a prophecy that he is to become king changes his life, and the lives of his fellow–Scots, as he embarks on a course of evil.

The means by which this transformation is achieved would have fascinated Shakespeare's contemporary audience, who were intrigued by – and fearful of – the supernatural. Today's audience takes less literally the witches, the apparitions, the ghost and the 'air-drawn' dagger, but appreciates the notion of the supernatural and the reality of the driving force of ambition.

Once Macbeth's course of action is established (committing a series of evil acts because his ambition has been stirred by the supernatural) Shakespeare hints to the audience what Macbeth's fate will be; who will be responsible for making sure that he pays for his crimes. Most of the scenes in the last two acts of the play are concerned with structuring the action to bring Macbeth, eventually, face to face with justice.

# Shakespeare's theatre

Nowadays entertainment is piped into people's houses – TV, the internet and radio provide hundreds of different programme choices every day. But in Shakespeare's time, people went out to be entertained. If you lived in a city like London you could go to the theatre.

But it wasn't the kind of theatre we know today. There was no electricity and the only artificial lighting was candles or torches, so plays had to be watched in daylight. This meant that the main part of the theatre was open to the skies.

Many of Shakespeare's plays were performed at the Globe Theatre. A modern replica of the Globe now stands on London's Bankside, close to where the original was built. By visiting the Globe Theatre you can discover what it was like to go to the theatre in Shakespeare's time.

Once you were inside, you would see that the ground plan was more or less circular: in *Henry V*, Shakespeare talks about 'the wooden O'. All around the outside were galleries where people could pay to sit on a wooden bench. From the galleries you looked down on the stage and – very important – you were under cover if it rained!

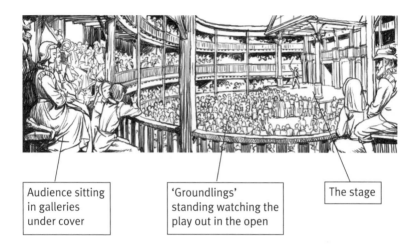

Audience sitting in galleries under cover

'Groundlings' standing watching the play out in the open

The stage

The stage measured about 12 metres by 12 metres. It was raised about 1.5 metres above the ground and was surrounded by a wide standing area. This was where the 'groundlings' went to watch the play. It was the cheapest way of seeing a play, but it meant that you had to stand for anything up to three hours. On the other hand you were much closer to the action – the people at the front were close enough to touch the actors when they came to the edge of the stage.

As you will see when you read the play, Shakespeare often gives the characters **soliloquies**, speeches which they speak when alone on stage. Often they seem to be deliberately sharing their thoughts with the audience. When you look at the stage of the Globe and see how close the audience was, you realise how effective this must have been.

Some modern theatres have a curtain which hides the stage from the audience before the play and between scenes. This makes it easy to change the scenery without the audience seeing what is going on. In Shakespeare's theatre there was no curtain to conceal the main stage; the stage was always open to the audience. Very little scenery was used and if furniture was needed, the actors had to carry it on themselves. Similarly, if a character died on stage, the body had to be carried off as part of the action.

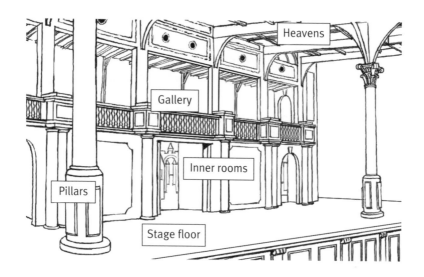

The stage was, however, quite complicated. Two large pillars on the main lower stage supported the roof, which was known as the 'heavens'. This kept the actors dry if it rained, but it could also be used for the action of the play. In some of the plays Shakespeare has characters lowered from above down onto the stage. There were also trapdoors in the stage itself, so that people could suddenly appear from below. The heavens contained a space which could be used for sound effects. Cannons could be fired for battle scenes and cannon balls rolled along the floor to make the sound of thunder. At the back of the stage there was an inner room which could be concealed by a curtain. This was sometimes used for short scenes in the play. The gallery could be used by musicians, or as an additional acting area.

# Shakespeare's language

It is easy to look at the text of this play and say to yourself, 'I'm never going to understand that!' but it is important not to be put off. Remember that there are two reasons why Shakespeare's language may seem strange at first:

1  He was writing 400 years ago and the English language has changed over the centuries.

2  He wrote mainly in **verse**. As a result he sometimes changed the order of words to make them fit the verse form, and he used a large number of 'tricks of the trade': figures of speech and other techniques.

## Language change

This can cause three main kinds of problem:

### *Grammar*

Since the end of the sixteenth century, there have been some changes in English grammar. Some examples:

*Thee*, *thou*, *thy*, and the verb forms that go with them:

> **Thou wouldst** *be great,*
> *Art not without ambition, but without*
> *The illness should attend it. What* **thou wouldst** *highly,*
> *That* **wouldst thou** *holily;* **wouldst** *not play false,*
> *And yet* **wouldst** *wrongly win.*

Words contract (shorten) in different ways. For example:

> *'tis* rather than *it's*
> *who is't* for *who is it*

So we get a line like this:

> *If it were done when* **'tis** *done, then* **'twere** *well*
> *It were done quickly.*

Some of the 'little words' are different. For example: *an* for *if*.

## Words that have changed their meaning

Sometimes you will come across words that you think you know, but then discover that they don't mean what you expect them to mean. For example: *saucy* (Act 3 scene 4 line 24) meant *insulting, insolent* in Shakespeare's day. Now it means *cheeky*. Nowadays if something is *portable* it means that it is easy to carry around. But in Act 4 scene 3 line 89, it means something that *can be tolerated*.

## Words that have gone out of use

These are the most obvious and most frequent causes of difficulty. Shakespeare had – and used – a huge vocabulary. He loved using words, and pushing them to their limits. So you will come across many words you have not met before. These are explained in the notes on the page facing the play text.

# Verse and prose

Most of *Macbeth* is in **blank verse**, but parts are in **prose** and short sections are in **rhymed verse**.

## Blank verse

The main part of the play is written in lines of ten syllables, with a repeated even pattern of weak and strong 'beats':

*Till **Birnam wood** re**move** to **Dun**si**nane***
(ti **tum** ti **tum** ti **tum** ti **tum** ti **tum**)

The line divides into five sections, each with a weak and a strong beat. This is called an **iambic pentameter**.

If Shakespeare had made every line exactly the same, the play would soon become very monotonous, so he varies the **rhythm** in a number of ways. Often he just changes the pattern of weak and strong slightly:

*His **sil**ver **skin laced** with his **gold**en **blood***
(ti **tum** ti **tum tum** ti ti **tum** ti **tum**)

In some parts of the play the variations are much more frequent and obvious. For example, try reading this speech aloud to see the effect it can have:

> She should have died hereafter;
> There would have been a time for such a word.
> Tomorrow, and tomorrow, and tomorrow,
> Creeps in this petty pace from day to day,
> To the last syllable of recorded time;
> And all our yesterdays have lighted fools
> The way to dusty death. Out, out, brief candle!
> Life's but a walking shadow, a poor player,
> That struts and frets his hour upon the stage,
> And then is heard no more. It is a tale
> Told by an idiot, full of sound and fury,
> Signifying nothing.

So the verse of the play has a strong but varied **rhythm**. Most of the lines do not rhyme, so they are 'blank' – hence the term blank verse.

## Rhymed verse

Sometimes Shakespeare uses a pattern of rhymed lines. In *Macbeth* scenes quite often end with pairs of lines that rhyme:

> If this which he avouches does ap**pear**,
> There is nor flying hence, nor tarrying **here**.
>
> I 'gin to be aweary of the **sun**,
> And wish th' estate o' th' world were now un**done**.
>
> Ring the alarum bell! Blow wind, come **wrack**,
> At least we'll die with harness on our **back**.
> (Act 5 scene 5 lines 47–52)

This use of rhyming couplets helps to round the scene off and gives the ending a musical quality.

## Prose

Most of *Macbeth* is in verse, but there are some sections written in 'ordinary' sentences: prose. Some characters in the play speak only in prose – for example, the Porter. Some characters speak verse at times and prose at others, depending on the situation. So for example in Act 1 scene 5 Lady Macbeth reads her husband's letter, which is in prose, and then comments on it, and him, in verse.

# Macbeth

## Characters

MACBETH, Thane of Glamis, later Thane of Cawdor and
    King of Scotland

LADY MACBETH, his wife

DUNCAN, King of Scotland *weak?*

MALCOLM, his older son *Good king, strategic, happy ending.*

DONALBAIN, his younger son *meh*

BANQUO, a Thane *he's not Macbeth → doesn't turn to the dark side*

FLEANCE, Banquo's son *Future king.*

MACDUFF, Thane of Fife *nemesis → saves Scotland for revenge*

LADY MACDUFF, his wife *Serves to punishes Macbeth.*

SON of Macduff *dies — end Macduff's lineage. Make him feel guilty.*

ROSS, a Thane

LENNOX, a Thane

MENTEITH, a Thane

ANGUS, a Thane

CAITHNESS, a Thane

GENTLEWOMAN, Lady Macbeth's attendant *Doctor needs somebody to talk to.*

SEYTON, Macbeth's armour bearer *For Macbeth.*

PORTER at Macbeth's castle *clown, comic relief*

CAPTAIN *To show how cool Macbeth is*

OLD MAN *Represents Scotland.*

Scottish DOCTOR } *Trust, clever, educated.*

ENGLISH DOCTOR }

Three MURDERERS

Three WITCHES *women screw up*

HECATE *doesn't appear*

Three other witches

Three APPARITIONS

SIWARD, Earl of Northumberland

YOUNG SIWARD, his son

Lords, soldiers, attendants, servants, and messengers

Scene: *Scotland and England*

Three witches immediately establish the influence of the supernatural.
They are to meet Macbeth when a battle is over.

| | |
|---|---|
| **SD** | ***Thunder and lightning*** In superstitious times it was believed that fierce storms released forces of evil, and were omens of unrest in individual people and whole countries. |
| **3** | **hurlyburly** fighting |
| **5** | **ere** before |
| **8** | **Greymalkin** The name of a grey cat; each witch had a familiar, an animal link with the spirit world. The familiars are calling to the witches. |
| **9** | **Paddock** A toad (another familiar) |
| | **Anon!** At once! |
| **10** | **Fair ... fair** To the witches, what is evil is good; what is good they find repulsive. |
| **11** | **Hover** A suggestion that the witches can somehow move through the air. |
| | **fog ... air** i.e. not the normal atmosphere when there is a thunderstorm |

Duncan, King of Scotland, meets a wounded captain.

| | |
|---|---|
| **SD** | ***Alarum*** Call to arms |
| **2** | **plight** condition |
| | **revolt** rebellion |

# Act One

*5 Acts ✱*

## Scene 1

*Thunder and lightning*  pathetic fallacy,
*Enter three* WITCHES  Supernatural

1ST WITCH   When shall we three meet again  playful rhyme.
            In thunder, lightning, or in rain?

2ND WITCH   When the hurlyburly's done,
            When the battle's lost and won.)  objectivity

3RD WITCH   That will be ere the set of sun.                    5

1ST WITCH   Where the place?

2ND WITCH                    Upon the heath.  Barren land

3RD WITCH   There to meet with Macbeth.

1ST WITCH   I come Greymalkin!  Creepy critters

2ND WITCH   Paddock calls.

3RD WITCH                    Anon!

ALL         (Fair is foul, and foul is fair;)  Deception; Appearance
            Hover through the fog and filthy air.  of reality.
            words of the witches,                  [*Exeunt*
            Lady Macbeth
            Malcolm.

## Scene 2

order of lineage

*Alarum within*  inside the stage
ENTER DUNCAN, MALCOLM, DONALBAIN, LENNOX, *with*
*attendants, meeting a bleeding* CAPTAIN
                good blood → war.
DUNCAN      What (bloody man) is that? He can report,
            As seemeth by his plight, of the revolt

Revolution in Scotland
Malcolm leads his group into battle
good king.

3

The wounded captain reports that Macbeth has defeated the rebellion of Highlanders and Islanders, led by Macdonald. No sooner was that battle over than Sweno, King of Norway, began an attack on the tired Scottish army.

| | |
|---|---|
| **3** | **sergeant** the wounded captain |
| **6** | **broil** battle |
| **8** | **spent** exhausted |
| **9** | **choke their art** prevent each other from swimming |
| **11** | **villainies** evil qualities |
| **12** | **Western Isles** Hebrides |
| **13** | **kerns and gallowglasses** Kerns were Irish foot-soldiers; gallowglasses were soldiers whose special duty was to the chieftain – their weapon of choice was the axe. |
| **14** | **fortune** Here, fortune is personified as someone who can take a hand in the action (**personification** – see Glossary p. 241). |
| **15** | **whore** mistress |
| | **all** everything that is set against him |
| **17** | **brandished steel** drawn sword |
| **18** | **smoked with bloody execution** steamed with blood |
| **19** | **valour's minion** bravery's favourite |
| **20** | **slave** (a contemptuous reference to Macdonald) |
| **21** | **Which** who (Macbeth) |
| **22** | **unseamed ... chops** split him open from the navel to the jaw |
| **24** | **cousin** Duncan and Macbeth were grandsons of King Malcolm, whom Duncan succeeded. |
| **25** | **reflection** shining |
| **27–8** | **So ... swells** at the moment of triumph further danger arises |
| **29** | **justice** the claim that they have right on their side |
| **30** | **skipping** quick-footed |
| **31** | **Norwegian lord** Sweno, King of Norway |
| | **surveying vantage** seeing his chance |
| **32** | **furbished** well-polished, well-prepared |

The newest state. *) He doesn't know what's happening.*

MALCOLM          This is the sergeant
Who, like a good and hardy soldier fought
'Gainst my captivity. Hail brave friend.      5
Say to the King the knowledge of the broil
As thou didst leave it.

CAPTAIN          Doubtful it stood,
*Clinging to each other.* (As two spent swimmers, that do cling together
And choke their art.) The merciless Macdonald –
(Worthy to be a rebel) for to that *He deserves bad* 10
The multiplying villainies of nature
Do swarm upon him – from the Western Isles
Of kerns and gallowglasses is supplied,
And fortune on his damned quarrel smiling
*1st time* Showed like a rebel's whore. But all's too weak,    15
*he's respected* (For brave Macbeth) – well he deserves that name –
Disdaining fortune, with his brandished steel,
(Which smoked with bloody execution,) *Good blood bc.*
Like valour's minion ) *Brave, respect* *he kills a rebel.*
Carved out his passage, till he faced (the slave;) *Just* 20
Which ne'er shook hands, nor bade farewell to *an insult.*
*Foreshadow! (Macbeth is beheaded.)* him,
(Till he unseamed him from the nave to the chops,) *Jaw Until he killed him.*
And fixed his head upon our battlements.

DUNCAN   O valiant cousin, worthy gentleman! *Family*

CAPTAIN   As whence the sun 'gins his reflection      25
Shipwrecking storms and direful thunders break,
So from that spring, whence comfort seemed to
     come,
Discomfort swells. Mark King of Scotland, mark.
No sooner justice had, with valour armed,
Compelled these skipping kerns to trust their
     heels,      30
*Scotland attacked again.* But the Norwegian lord, surveying vantage,
With furbished arms, and new supplies of men,
Began a fresh assault.

The captain continues, telling how Macbeth and Banquo led their men with renewed vigour. At this point the captain collapses from his wounds and is taken for treatment. Ross completes the tale of the victory against the Norwegians.

**33–4**    **Dismayed ... Banquo?** Did this not make Macbeth and Banquo feel dismay?

**35**    **As sparrows ... lion** In the same way that sparrows dismay eagles, or the hare dismays the lion; this is an example of **irony** (see Glossary p. 241).

**36**    **If I say sooth** To tell the truth

**37**    **cracks** charges of gunpowder

**39**    **Except** Unless

      **reeking** steaming

**40**    **memorise** make memorable, famous

      **Golgotha** 'the place of the skull' (where Jesus Christ was crucified)

**44**    **smack of** suggest

**45**    **Thane** A Scottish title, roughly equivalent to an earl.

**47**    **seems to** is about to

**49**    **flout** mock

**50**    **fan our people cold** make our people shiver with fear

**53**    **dismal** disastrous

**54**    **Bellona's bridegroom** Mars, the Roman god of war, was husband to Bellona.

      **lapped in proof** clad in armour

**55**    **Confronted ... self-comparisons** matched him in every way

**57**    **Curbing** restraining

      **lavish** insolent

DUNCAN                              Dismayed not this
                    Our captains, (Macbeth and Banquo?) Both leaders.

CAPTAIN                                     Yes, Animal
                    As sparrows eagles, or the hare the lion.   image:   35
                    If I say sooth, I must report they were   Powerful, brave.
*force*             As cannons overcharged with double cracks,
*Traitor: trouble*  So they doubly redoubled strokes upon the foe.
*comes from*        Except they meant to bathe in reeking wounds,
*within.*           Or memorise another Golgotha,                40
*ord king!*         I cannot tell –
*trouble comes*     But I am faint, my gashes cry for help.
*from out.*
DUNCAN              So well thy words become thee, as thy wounds,
                    They smack of honour both. Go get him surgeons.

                                        [*Exit* CAPTAIN, *attended*

                    *Enter* ROSS *and* ANGUS

                    Who comes here?

MALCOLM                             The worthy Thane of Ross.      45

LENNOX              What a haste looks through his eyes! So should
                       he look
                    That seems to speak things strange.

ROSS                                        God save the King!

DUNCAN              Whence cam'st thou, worthy Thane?

ROSS                                        From Fife, great King,
                    Where the Norwegian banners flout the sky,
                    And fan our people cold.                       50
                    Norway himself, with terrible numbers,
                    Assisted by that most disloyal traitor,
*executed &*        (The Thane of Cawdor,) began a dismal conflict,
*Macbeth gets*      Till that Bellona's bridegroom, lapped in proof,
*his job*           Confronted him with self-comparisons,          55
                    Point against point, rebellious arm 'gainst arm,
                    Curbing his lavish spirit; and, to conclude,

7

Duncan pronounces the death sentence on the treacherous Thane of
Cawdor, and says that Macbeth shall now have that title.

**59**    **craves composition** begs for peace terms
**60**    **deign** allow
**61**    **disbursed** paid up
       **Saint Colme's Inch** Inchcolm (an island in the Firth of Forth)
**62**    **dollars** These were sixteenth-century, not eleventh-century, coins.
**64**    **bosom** dearest, closest
       **present** immediate

Whilst awaiting the arrival of Macbeth, the witches discuss their spiteful
treatment of a sea-captain.

**2**    **Killing swine** Witches were often held responsible for the death
of animals.
**5**    **'Aroint thee'** Get lost!
       **rump-fed ronyon** fat-bottomed hag; the woman has responded
fearlessly to the witch. Perhaps a religious belief makes her
confident that evil will not affect her. However, the witch decides
to take out her spite on the woman's husband.
**7**    **sieve** A vessel that witches were believed to use.
**8**    **a rat ... tail** The witch will turn herself into an animal, but an
incomplete one.
**9**    **I'll do** I'll take revenge

The victory fell on us. *Macbeth wins.*

DUNCAN                                    Great happiness!

ROSS                                          That now Sweno,
The Norways' King, craves composition.) *Thanks to Macbeth.*
Nor would we deign him burial of his men               60
Till he disbursed, at Saint Colme's Inch,
Ten thousand dollars to our general use.

DUNCAN   No more that Thane of Cawdor shall deceive
Our bosom interest. Go pronounce his present
        death,  *Foreshadow*
And with his former title greet Macbeth.               65

ROSS     I'll see it done.  *Bc it's mentioned now, can be argued that witches don't see the*

DUNCAN   What he hath lost noble Macbeth hath won.  *future.*

                                          [*Exeunt*


## Scene 3

*Thunder*  *Special effects.*

*Enter three* WITCHES

1ST WITCH   Where hast thou been, sister?  *Following tradition*

2ND WITCH   Killing swine.

3RD WITCH               Sister, where thou?

1ST WITCH   A sailor's wife had chestnuts in her lap,
And munched, and munched, and munched –
        'Give me,' quoth I.
'Aroint thee witch,' the rump-fed ronyon cries.        5
Her husband's to Aleppo gone, master o' th' *Tiger*, *Ship*
But in a sieve I'll thither sail,
And like a rat without a tail,
I'll do, I'll do, and I'll do. ) *I'll take revenge*

2ND WITCH   I'll give thee a wind.  *Say it 3 times*        10

                        *witches go by 3s*

9

The witches continue their story. Macbeth and Banquo enter on their way to report to Duncan at Forres.

**13–16** **I myself ... card** I control the other winds and know which ports they blow on from every point of the compass

**16** **shipman's card** The compass-card on which the 32 points of the compass are marked.

**17** **dry as hay** (so he will not be able to put in to port for water)

**18–19** **Sleep ... lid** he will not be able to fall asleep at all

**19** **penthouse lid** eyelid

**20** **forbid** accursed

**21** **sev'n-nights ... nine** Seven nights is a week, and nine was considered to be a magic number.

**22** **peak, and pine** waste away

**23** **bark** ship

**27** **pilot's thumb** Parts of corpses were used in casting spells.

**32** **Posters** speedy travellers

**34** **Thrice** The number three and multiples of three have long been regarded as special numbers – even magic ones.

**37** **So ... day** Macbeth could be referring 1) to the weather 2) to the victories.

**39** **attire** clothing

**41** **aught** anything

**41–2** **aught ... question** any creatures that a human being may interrogate

| 1ST WITCH | Th' art kind. |
|---|---|
| 3RD WITCH | And I another. |

1ST WITCH  I myself have all the other,
And the very ports they blow,      *They'll control*
All the quarters that they know    *the elements.* 15
I' the shipman's card.

*Sexuality ?*  I'll drain him dry as hay;
Sleep shall neither night nor day  *Torture, not*
Hang upon his penthouse lid.       *sleeping*
He shall live a man forbid; 20
Weary sev'n-nights nine times nine  *Association to 3*
Shall he dwindle, peak, and pine.   *complicated plan.*
Though his bark cannot be lost,
Yet it shall be tempest-tossed.
Look what I have. 25

2ND WITCH  Show me, show me.

1ST WITCH  Here I have a pilot's thumb,       *Superstition*
Wrecked as homeward he did come.

*A*            *IV, i, 44*   [*Drum within*   *OFF stage.*
3RD WITCH  A drum, a drum!      *drums.*
                                *↳ war instruments*
Macbeth doth come.               *make him* 30 *a*
                                 *warrior.*

ALL  The Weird sisters, hand in hand,
Posters of the sea and land,
Thus do go about, about,
Thrice to thine, and thrice to mine,
And thrice again, to make up nine. 35
Peace, the charm's wound up.

*Enter* MACBETH *and* BANQUO

MACBETH  So foul and fair a day I have not seen.  ) *Echoes the*
                                                    *witches from the*
BANQUO  How far is't called to Forres? What are these,  *beggining.*
So withered, and so wild in their attire,
That look not like th' inhabitants o' th' earth,)  *Supernatural,*
And yet are on't? Live you, or are you aught
That man may question? You seem to understand
                me,   *Banquo doubts them*

11

Each witch greets Macbeth differently: Thane of Glamis, Thane of Cawdor and 'that shalt be King hereafter'. Banquo asks what the witches have to say to him. They tell Banquo that his descendants will be kings. Macbeth tries to question the witches.

| | |
|---|---|
| 43 | **choppy** chapped |
| 49 | **hereafter** in the future |
| 50 | **start** Macbeth has made a slight movement of surprise or alarm. |
| 52 | **fantastical** imaginary |
| 54-5 | **present ... hope** amazing predictions of good fortune |
| 56 | **rapt withal** carried away with it |
| 57-8 | **look ... will not** see how things are going to develop |
| 66 | **get** beget, be the ancestor of |
| 69 | **imperfect speakers** They are imperfect because they have left things unspoken. |
| 70 | **Sinel** (Macbeth's father) |
| 72 | **prosperous** thriving, healthy |
| 73 | **prospect of belief** realms of possibility |
| 75 | **owe** get |
| | **intelligence** information |

By each at once her choppy finger laying
Upon her skinny lips. You should be women,
And yet your beards forbid me to interpret          45
That you are so.

MACBETH                              Speak if you can. What are you? *Dramatic irony.*

1ST WITCH    All hail Macbeth, hail to thee, Thane of Glamis!

2ND WITCH    All hail Macbeth, hail to thee, Thane of Cawdor! *They're right*

3RD WITCH    All hail Macbeth, that shalt be King hereafter!

BANQUO       Good sir, why do you start, and seem to fear      50 *jump*
*Macbeth turns evil.* Things that do sound so fair? I' th' name of truth
Are ye fantastical, or that indeed
Which outwardly ye show? My noble partner
*we only hear about good guy Macbeth* You greet with present grace, and great prediction
Of noble having, and of royal hope,                 55
That he seems rapt withal. To me you speak not.
If you can look into the seeds of time,
And say which grain will grow, and which will not,
Speak then to me, who neither beg nor fear
Your favours nor your hate. *he doesn't care,* 60
                                    *not like Macbeth.*

1ST WITCH    Hail!

2ND WITCH    Hail!      3

3RD WITCH    Hail!          *prediction:*

1ST WITCH    Lesser than Macbeth, and greater. *honour*
*nobility*

2ND WITCH    Not so happy, yet much happier. *go to heaven* 65
*killed*

3RD WITCH    Thou shalt get kings, though thou be none. *beget, children*
So all hail Macbeth and Banquo!

1ST WITCH    Banquo and Macbeth, all hail!
                *not telling proper truth.*

MACBETH      Stay you imperfect speakers, tell me more.
*Dad.* By Sinel's death I know I am Thane of Glamis,   70
*He didn't kill him* But how of Cawdor? The Thane of Cawdor lives
A prosperous gentleman, and to be king
Stands not within the prospect of belief,
No more than to be Cawdor. Say from whence
You owe this strange intelligence, or why           75

13

The witches disappear. Macbeth and Banquo begin to discuss what has happened. Ross and Angus enter and Macbeth learns that he is now the Thane of Cawdor.

**76**     **blasted** blighted

**77**     **charge** command

**78–9**   **The earth ... them** They disappear like air-bubbles

**80**     **corporal** to be flesh

**81**     **Would** I wish

**83**     **insane root** root of a plant which causes hallucinations

**87**     **selfsame** exactly the same

**91**     **personal venture** own feats of bravery

**92–3**   **His wonders ... or his** These are confusing lines, but what is clear is that the king's mind is in turmoil at the amazing events of the day.

**93**     **Silenced with that** This conflict in his mind has made him speechless

**96**     **Nothing ... make** you were not at all afraid of what you were having to do

**97**     **Strange ... death** unnatural forms of death

**98**     **post with post** messenger after messenger

**100**    **poured** the praise flooded in

**102**    **herald** accompany

**104**    **earnest** pledge

Upon this blasted heath you stop our way
With such prophetic greeting. Speak, I charge you.

*Tries to command.*

[WITCHES *vanish*

BANQUO    The earth hath bubbles, as the water has,
          And these are of them. Whither are they vanished?

MACBETH   Into the air; and what seem'd corporal melted          80
          As breath into the wind. Would they had stayed.

BANQUO    Were such things here as we do speak about?
          Or have we eaten on the insane root          *Smoking*
          That takes the reason prisoner?          *questioning*
                                                      *beliefs.*

MACBETH   Your children shall be kings.

BANQUO                          You shall be King.          85

MACBETH   And Thane of Cawdor too; went it not so?    *wants to talk*

BANQUO    To th' selfsame tune and words. Who's here?

          *Enter* ROSS *and* ANGUS

ROSS      The King hath happily received, Macbeth,    *Macbeth's*
          The news of thy success; and when he reads   *a hero.*
                                                        90
          Thy personal venture in the rebels' fight,
          His wonders and his praises do contend,
          Which should be thine or his. Silenced with that,
          In viewing o'er the rest o' th' selfsame day,
*Betrayal* He finds thee in the stout Norwegian ranks,          95
          Nothing afeard of what thyself didst make,   *Brave*
          Strange images of death. As thick as hail
          Came post with post, and every one did bear
          Thy praises in his kingdom's great defence,
          And poured them down before him.

ANGUS                                   We are sent          100
          To give thee from our royal master thanks,
          Only to herald thee into his sight,
          Not pay thee.    *promise of great honour*

ROSS      And for an earnest of a greater honour,   *Supernatural*
          He bade me, from him, call thee Thane of  *Thinks of being*
          Cawdor;    *prophecy comes true*          105    *King.*
          *spooky*

Banquo and Macbeth are shocked. Banquo warns Macbeth that evil is at work. Even though the predictions seem favourable at the moment, there is something sinister about them. Macbeth begins to consider what it will mean if the third prediction is to come true.

**106**      **addition** fresh title

**108–9**      **dress … robes** give me another man's clothes to wear

**110**      **heavy judgement** sentence of death

**111**      **was combined** joined forces

**112**      **line** give support to

**113**      **vantage** benefit

**114**      **wrack** ruin

**115**      **capital** deserving the death penalty

**117**      **behind** still to come

**120**      **trusted home** believed absolutely

**121**      **enkindle you unto** make you desire

**122**      **But 'tis strange** It is unnatural, supernatural

**123–6**      **oftentimes … consequence** the forces of evil encourage us to bring about our own destruction, by giving us accurate information about things which are trivial, while misleading us on important matters

**127**      **Cousins** Friends

     **a word I pray you** Banquo is taking Ross and Angus to one side.

**128–9**      **happy … theme** promising forerunners to the increasing splendour of the royal story

**130**      **soliciting** prompting

**132**      **earnest** promise

In which addition, hail most worthy Thane,
For it is thine.

*represents a whisper*

BANQUO [*Aside*] What, can the devil speak true?

*supernatural* · *Typical association of witches with the devil*

MACBETH The Thane of Cawdor lives. Why do you dress me
In borrowed robes? ) *Incredulous?*

ANGUS *don't belong* Who was the Thane lives yet,

*not reality* But under heavy judgement bears that life          110
(Which he deserves to lose.) Whether he was
combined *like Macbeth at the end.*

*Thane is a traitor*

With those of Norway, or did line the rebel
With hidden help and vantage, or that with both
He laboured in his country's wrack, I know not;
But treasons capital, confessed and proved,          115
Have overthrown him.

*Traitors deserve to die.*

MACBETH [*Aside*] Glamis, and Thane of Cawdor.

*His ambitions grow*

The greatest is behind. [*To* ROSS *and* ANGUS] Thanks
for your pains. *They think it's his peak.*
[*To* BANQUO] (Do you not hope your children shall
be kings,
When those that gave the Thane of Cawdor to me
Promised no less to them?) *Believes the witches*

BANQUO That, trusted home,          120

*Voice of reason*

Might yet enkindle you unto the crown,
Besides the Thane of Cawdor. (But 'tis strange:)

*Doesn't fully believe yet.*

*manipulation* And oftentimes, to win us to our harm,
(The instruments of darkness) tell us truths,

*supernatural*

Win us with honest trifles, to betray's          125
In deepest consequence. *Fair is foul*

*guys* Cousins, a word I pray you. *Foul is fair.*

MACBETH [*Aside*] (Two truths are told) *Glamis & Cawdor.*

*Ambition grows more*

As happy prologues to the swelling act
Of the imperial theme. – I thank you gentlemen. –
[*Aside*] This supernatural soliciting          130
Cannot be ill, cannot be good.
If ill, why hath it given me earnest of success,
Commencing in a truth? I am Thane of Cawdor.

Macbeth decides to let the future take care of itself, and he and Banquo agree to discuss matters at a more convenient time.

| | |
|---|---|
| **134** | **yield** give in |
| | **suggestion** temptation |
| **135** | **horrid ... hair** horrifying concept makes my hair stand on end |
| **136** | **my seated ... ribs** my heart, normally settled in its place, beat against my ribs |
| **137** | **Against ... nature** unnaturally |
| | **Present fears** Real causes of fear |
| **139–41** | **My thought ... surmise** Murder is only a thought going through my mind, and yet I am so shaken by it that I am unable to act |
| **141–2** | **nothing ... not** the only thing that is real for me is what is going on inside my head |
| **142** | **rapt** absorbed |
| **144** | **Without my stir** without my having to do anything about it |
| **145–6** | **Like ... use** just as new clothes do not fit properly until they have been worn for a time |
| **146–7** | **Come ... day** However stormy the weather may be, life goes on |
| **148** | **we ... leisure** we are waiting until you are ready |
| **149** | **favour** pardon |
| | **wrought** troubled |
| **150** | **things forgotten** things I was trying to remember |
| **151–2** | **where ... them** where they are constantly, as I turn the pages of my memory |
| **153** | **hath chanced** happened |
| **154** | **The interim ... it** once we have had time to consider this matter |
| **155** | **Out free hearts** frankly |

*[handwritten: sychological trauma]*

If good, why do I yield to (that suggestion,) *[handwritten: murder]*
Whose horrid image doth unfix my hair,                               135
And make my seated heart knock at my ribs,
(Against the use of nature?) Present fears *[handwritten: Un-natural]*.
Are less than horrible imaginings.

*[handwritten: starts to have evil thoughts]*

My thought, whose murder yet is but fantastical,)
(Shakes so my single state of man, that function      140
Is smothered in surmise, and nothing is      *[handwritten: Everything's]*
But what is not. ) *[handwritten: Horrified at himself?]* *[handwritten: confusing.]*

BANQUO                    Look how our partner's rapt.

                                                    *[handwritten: character]*
MACBETH    [*Aside*] If chance will have me King, why chance *[handwritten: gets]*
*[handwritten: ambition makes him do it.]* (may crown me *[handwritten: doesn't really want to be]* *[handwritten: chance to]*
           Without my stir. ) *[handwritten: evil. Fate → he believes.]* *[handwritten: escape.]*

BANQUO                    New honours come upon him,
           Like our strange garments, cleave not to their
              mould                  *[handwritten: excuses Macbeth's]*      145
           But with the aid of use.      *[handwritten: psycho behaviour?]*

MACBETH    [*Aside*]                    Come what come may, *[handwritten: important]*
*[handwritten: Decision. "whatever"]* Time and the hour runs through the roughest day.

BANQUO     Worthy Macbeth, we stay upon your leisure.

MACBETH    Give me your favour: my dull brain was wrought
           With things forgotten. Kind gentlemen, your pains  150
           Are registered where every day I turn
           The leaf to read them. Let us toward the King.
           [*To* BANQUO] Think upon what hath chanced, and at
*[handwritten: pretends that he wants to be king talk]* more time,
           (The interim having weighed it, let us speak) *[handwritten: but]*
           (Our free hearts each to other. ) *[handwritten: doesn't]*

BANQUO                         Very gladly.           155

MACBETH    Till then enough. – Come friends.

                                              [*Exeunt*

19

# Act 1 scenes 1 to 3

## Who's who

At the beginning of *Macbeth* we meet a lot of different people and we hear reports of several more. We have to work out who they all are and think about how they are going to fit into the story. In Act 1 scene 2:

- we meet seven characters
- another five characters are mentioned.

One way of getting a grip on who's who is to divide the characters into groups. We can group these characters like this:

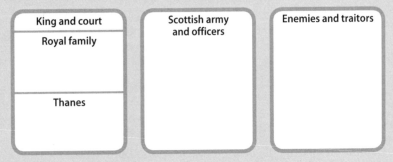

King and court

Royal family

Thanes

Scottish army and officers

Enemies and traitors

### Work with a partner

1  Make a list of the named characters who appear in scene 2.

2  Add to the list the names of other characters who are mentioned in the scene.

3  Look at the list of characters on page 1 to see what other information you can find about these characters.

4  Copy out the diagram and write the name of each character in the right group.

## What happened?

### Work on your own

1  Draw a picture of what you think scene 1 looks like.

2  In scene 2 we find out what happens in a battle. The seven sentences in boxes opposite sum up the story. Write them down in the order in which they are reported.

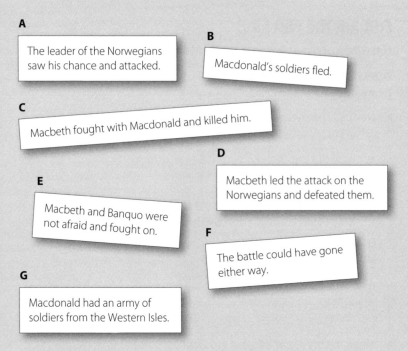

**A**

The leader of the Norwegians saw his chance and attacked.

**B**

Macdonald's soldiers fled.

**C**

Macbeth fought with Macdonald and killed him.

**D**

Macbeth led the attack on the Norwegians and defeated them.

**E**

Macbeth and Banquo were not afraid and fought on.

**F**

The battle could have gone either way.

**G**

Macdonald had an army of soldiers from the Western Isles.

**3** Now look at scene 3.

Copy and complete the table to show what happens in this scene:

| Characters | Summary | Details | |
|---|---|---|---|
| Three Witches | First Witch tells a story | The story is about... | |
| Three Witches Macbeth Banquo | The Witches give Macbeth three titles. The Witches make Banquo three promises. | Macbeth's titles: 1 2 3 | Banquo's promises: 1 2 3 |
| Macbeth Banquo Ross Angus | Angus gives Macbeth some good news. Macbeth has some nasty thoughts. | The good news: | The nasty thoughts: |

# Filming the witches

The witches appear in scene 1 and scene 3.

**Work in a group of three or four**

1 Read scene 1, and scene 3 lines 1–36.

2 Discuss these questions:

   a What do you think these three women looked like?

   b How did they move?

   c How did they speak?

3 Suppose you were making a film of the witch scenes.

   a How could you show the witches?

   b Would you use sound effects?

   c Would you use music?

   d What other special effects could you use?

4 Divide the scene between the members of the group, so that each person has about 10–15 lines to work on.

5 Make a storyboard for your group of lines. Build up a picture in your mind of what people can see and hear as each line is spoken.

6 Set out your ideas in a storyboard. For example, we could make a storyboard for the beginning of scene 3 like this:

| Lines | Actions | Visual effects | Sound/music |
|-------|---------|----------------|-------------|
| 1–2 | At first we can see nothing. Then slowly the shapes of the three witches appear out of the mist. | Swirling mist | Thunder mixed with 'Witches' theme music |
| | | | |

7 When you have all finished, pass your storyboards around the group.

8 Prepare a short report for the rest of the class explaining how you have approached filming these two scenes.

# Quotation quiz

For each of these quotations, work out:

1 who said it

2 who they were speaking to

3 what it tells us about

   **a** the speaker

   **b** the situation

   **c** any other characters.

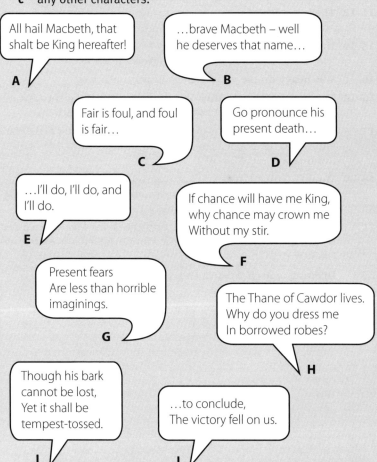

All hail Macbeth, that shalt be King hereafter!

**A**

…brave Macbeth – well he deserves that name…

**B**

Fair is foul, and foul is fair…

**C**

Go pronounce his present death…

**D**

…I'll do, I'll do, and I'll do.

**E**

If chance will have me King, why chance may crown me Without my stir.

**F**

Present fears Are less than horrible imaginings.

**G**

The Thane of Cawdor lives. Why do you dress me In borrowed robes?

**H**

Though his bark cannot be lost, Yet it shall be tempest-tossed.

**I**

…to conclude, The victory fell on us.

**J**

The Thane of Cawdor has been executed. Duncan thanks Macbeth profusely for his part in the victories. Macbeth modestly says that he was only doing his duty.

| | |
|---|---|
| **2** | **in commission** who were given the responsibility of making sure that the sentence was carried out |
| **8** | **Became him like** was as honourable as |
| **9** | **been ... death** thought deeply about how to die |
| **10** | **owed** owned |
| **11** | **careless trifle** trivial thing of no importance |
| **11–12** | **There's ... face** There is no way to judge how a man thinks from how he looks |
| **13–14** | **He was ... trust** In view of the way Macbeth's thoughts are driving him, this is **dramatic irony** (see Glossary p. 239). |
| **16** | **Was heavy on me** was weighing heavily upon me |
| **16–18** | **Thou art ... overtake thee** Your value to me is so far ahead of me, that however hard I try to repay you, I cannot catch up |
| **17** | **swiftest wing** Duncan is making it clear that the fastest flight of a bird would still not be enough to bring Macbeth's reward to him (for **imagery** see Glossary p. 240). |
| **18–20** | **Would ... mine** If only you had deserved less of me I might have been able to repay you in the way you deserve. (But because you deserve so much, that is impossible.) |
| **21** | **'More ... pay'** You deserve more than everything I have. Since this is what the witches have prophesied for Macbeth this is **irony** (see Glossary p. 241). |
| **23** | **In doing ... itself** are their own reward |

## Scene 4

*Flourish*

*Enter* DUNCAN, MALCOLM, DONALBAIN, LENNOX, *and attendants*

DUNCAN    Is execution done on Cawdor? Are not
Those in commission yet returned?

*[handwritten: Foreshadowing — execution will happen in Cawdor.]*

MALCOLM                          My liege,
They are not yet come back. But I have spoke
With one that saw him die, who did report
That very frankly he confessed his treasons,      5
Implored your Highness' pardon, and set forth
A deep repentance. Nothing in his life
Became him like the leaving it. He died
As one that had been studied in his death
To throw away the dearest thing he owed      10
As 'twere a careless trifle.

*[handwritten: Gruesome?]*

DUNCAN                          There's no art
To find the mind's construction in the face.
He was a gentleman on whom I built
An absolute trust.

*[handwritten: Appearance might be misleading. Doesn't think he's a traitor.]*

*[handwritten margin: D.1: trusts Cawdor — He's a traitor. Trusts Macbeth — kills him.]*

*Enter* MACBETH, BANQUO, ROSS, *and* ANGUS

*[handwritten: Dramatic Irony.]*

                          O worthiest cousin,
The sin of my ingratitude even now      15
Was heavy on me. Thou art so far before,
That swiftest wing of recompense is slow
To overtake thee. Would thou hadst less deserved,
That the proportion both of thanks and payment
Might have been mine. Only I have left to say,      20
'More is thy due than more than all can pay.'

*[handwritten: "you deserve more"]*

*[handwritten margin: pretends to be humble so people are loyal to him.]*

*[handwritten: Thanks people ↓ They like him]*

MACBETH    The service and the loyalty I owe,
In doing it pays itself. Your Highness' part
Is to receive our duties, and our duties

*[handwritten: - By thanking him in this way, Duncan gives Macbeth motivation to kill him]*

Duncan names Malcolm as his successor, and then invites himself to
Macbeth's castle. Macbeth sees that 'chance' will not make him king, and
he makes up his mind to do something about it.

**26–7**   **Which ... honour** which do only what they should to protect
your safety and so deserve your love and honour

**28–9**   **I have ... growing** I have begun to establish you and will do my
best to make you thrive

**30–1**   **That ... done so** you have deserved as much and this must be
equally recognised

**32–3**   **There ... own** If I flourish, you will benefit

**34**   **Wanton in fullness** full to overflowing

**34–5**   **seek ... sorrow** Duncan is so full of joy and gratitude that the
emotion turns to tears.

**37**   **We** The plural subject was often used by royalty in place of 'I'.

**establish ... upon** name as successor to the throne

**39**   **Prince of Cumberland** The title used for the heir to the Scottish
throne; by tradition, Duncan did not have to make his son his
successor.

**39–40**   **which honour ... only** he is not to be the only one to receive
honours

**41–2**   **But signs ... deservers** honours will be distributed widely to all
who deserve them

**44**   **The rest ... you** It is only a chore when I am not serving you

**45**   **harbinger** messenger

**45–6**   **make ... approach** delight my wife with the news that you are to
arrive

**48–9**   **that is ... o'erleap** Malcolm is an obstacle to the throne which will
either trip me up or which I must vault over

**50**   **Stars ... desires** Stars put out your light so that it will not see my
dark and wicked longings

**52**   **The eye ... hand** let the eye be blind to what the hand does

**52–3**   **yet let ... see** but let that thing happen which the eye is afraid to
see

*Offers loyalty*

Are to your throne and state, children and servants 25
Which do but what they should be doing every
  thing
Safe toward your love and honour.

*To honour their King*

DUNCAN                                      Welcome hither.

*manipulation*

I have begun to plant thee, and will labour
To make thee full of growing. Noble Banquo,
That hast no less deserved, nor must be known    30
No less to have done so. Let me infold thee,
And hold thee to my heart.                *Hug*

BANQUO                        There if I grow,
The harvest is your own.  *Thankful, Offers loyalty*

DUNCAN  *Crying of happiness.*  My plenteous joys,
Wanton in fullness, seek to hide themselves   *↓ Duncan's manipulation works*
*Tears →* In drops of sorrow. Sons, kinsmen, Thanes,   35
And you whose places are the nearest, know,

*Malcolm will be King*

We will establish our estate upon
Our eldest, Malcolm, whom we name hereafter
The Prince of Cumberland; which honour must
Not unaccompanied invest him only,             40
But signs of nobleness, like stars, shall shine
On all deservers. From hence to Inverness,
And bind us further to you.

MACBETH  The rest is labour, which is not used for you.
I'll be myself the harbinger, and make joyful   45
The hearing of my wife with your approach;
So humbly take my leave.

DUNCAN                            My worthy Cawdor.

MACBETH  [*Aside*] The Prince of Cumberland – that is a step,
On which I must fall down, or else o'erleap,
For in my way it lies. Stars hide your fires,     50
*Deception Hiding*  Let not light see my black and deep desires;  *I, v, 50*
The eye wink at the hand; yet let that be
Which the eye fears, when it is done to see.   *relates himself to darkness*
                                              [*Exit*

DUNCAN  True worthy Banquo; he is full so valiant,

**55**     **commendations** praises

**57**     **Whose ... before** who has gone to make preparations

**58**     **peerless** without equal

Lady Macbeth reads a letter from her husband, telling of the witches'
predictions. She knows Macbeth has ambition, but fears he is too noble to
make sure that the prediction is fulfilled.

**2**       **perfect'st report** most reliable information

**2–3**     **more ... knowledge** more knowledge than a human being can
           have

**4–5**     **made ... air** turned into air

**6**       **rapt** carried away with

           **missives** messengers

**8**       **before** already

**9**       **the coming ... time** the future

**11**      **deliver** tell

**12**      **the dues** your due share

**14**      **Lay ... heart** Keep it in your heart

**17**      **milk ... kindness** inner goodness

**18**      **catch ... way** adopt the most direct method

**18–20**   **Thou ... attend it** You want greatness, you do not lack ambition
           but you do not have the badness that needs to go with it

**20–1**    **What thou ... holily** You desire greatness by fair means

**21–2**    **wouldst not ... win** you don't want to cheat and yet you want to
           win unfairly

**22–3**    **Thou'dst ... have it** You want that thing which cries out 'This is
           how you must act if you are to achieve it'

**23**      **That** (the crown)

*praise Banquo*

And in his commendations I am fed.                                      55
It is a banquet to me. Let's after him,
Whose care is gone before to bid us welcome.
It is a peerless kinsman.

*Flourish. Exeunt*

## Scene 5

*Enter* LADY MACBETH, *reading a letter*   *& Solitary person.*

*Battle*

L. MACBETH  'They met me in the day of success; and I have
learned by the perfect'st report, they have more in *super natural*
them than mortal knowledge. When I burned in
*witches*  desire to question them further, they made *wants to know*
themselves air, into which they vanished. Whiles I   *5 more*
stood rapt in the wonder of it, came missives from
the King, who all-hailed me "Thane of Cawdor", by
which title, before these weird sisters saluted me,
and referred me to the coming on of time with
"Hail King that shalt be!" This have I thought         10
*queen*  good to deliver thee my dearest partner of
greatness, that thou mightst not lose the dues of
rejoicing by being ignorant of what greatness is   *one day*
*future* ( promised thee) Lay it to thy heart, and farewell.'
Glamis thou art, and Cawdor, and shalt be         15
*she believes the witches*  What thou art promised; yet do I fear thy nature,
It is too full o' th' milk of human kindness
To catch the nearest way. Thou wouldst be great,
*Murder.*  Art not without ambition, but without
The illness should attend it. What thou wouldst
highly,   *Do things the right way*   20
That wouldst thou holily; wouldst not play false,
And yet wouldst wrongly win. Thou'dst have,   *she makes him do it*
great Glamis,
That which cries 'Thus thou must do', if thou
have it,

Lady Macbeth is startled to learn that Duncan is on his way to the castle. She calls on the evil spirits to make her ruthless so that she can carry out the murder of Duncan.

**24–5**   **And that ... undone** the truth is more that you fear to do the deed than wish it did not need to be done (Lady Macbeth has realised instantly that the shortest route to the throne is murder and she cannot rely on Macbeth's firmness of purpose.)

**25**   **Hie thee hither** Hurry here to me

**27**   **chastise** whip

      **valour** boldness

**28**   **All ... thee** all that holds you back

      **golden round** crown

**29**   **metaphysical** supernatural

**32–3**   **Is not ... preparation** Isn't your master with him? If he were he would have let me know so that I could prepare

**35**   **had the ... him** rode faster than he did

**37**   **Give him tending** Look after him

**38**   **The raven ... hoarse** The croaking raven (a bird of ill-omen) is more hoarse than usual because it signals Duncan's death

**40–1**   **spirits ... thoughts** spirits that wait on 1) human thoughts 2) deadly thoughts ('mortal' carries both meanings)

**41**   **unsex me** take away my femininity, make me forget humanity

**43**   **direst** most bitter

**43–7**   **Make thick ... and it** Prevent pity from flowing in my veins, make sure that I can feel no compassion so that no feelings of humanity upset my ruthless intention, or stop me from carrying it out

**48**   **take ... gall** replace my milk with bitterness

      **murd'ring ministers** spirits of murder

**49**   **sightless substances** invisible state

**50**   **wait ... mischief** look after humanity's evil deeds

**51**   **pall thee** cover yourself

      **dunnest** darkest, murky

*Fear to act?*

And that which rather thou dost fear to do
Than wishest should be undone. Hie thee hither, 25
That I may pour my spirits in thine ear,  *Supernatural,*
And chastise with the valour of my tongue  *control.*
All that impedes thee from (the golden round,)  *crown.*
Which fate and (metaphysical aid) doth seem
To have thee crowned withal.  *Outside metaphysical world, supernatural.*

*Enter* MESSENGER

*Coincidence*
*good timing.*                    What is your tidings? 30

MESSENGER The King comes here tonight.

L. MACBETH                          Thou'rt mad to say it.
Is not thy master with him, who were't so
Would have informed for preparation.

MESSENGER So please you, it is true; our Thane is coming.
One of my fellows had the speed of him, 35
Who, almost dead for breath, had scarcely more
Than would make up his message.

L. MACBETH                          Give him tending;
He brings great news.  *dark*      [*Exit* MESSENGER
                    *Critter*
                    *death*   The raven himself is hoarse
That croaks the fatal entrance of Duncan
Under my battlements (Come you spirits  *Appeal to* 40
That tend on mortal thoughts) unsex me here,  *Witches*
And fill me from the crown to the toe top-full  *make me male ↗*
Of direst cruelty. Make thick my blood,  *male ↗*
Stop up th' access and passage to remorse,  *Strong cruel*
That no compunctious visitings of nature 45
Shake my (fell purpose) nor keep peace between
Th' effect and it. Come to my woman's breasts,  *Feminine motherhood*
And take my milk for gall, you murd'ring ministers,
Wherever in your sightless substances  *too weak to*
You wait on nature's mischief. (Come thick night, 50 *kill*
And pall thee in the dunnest smoke of hell,  *without Spirits*

*manly, evil*
*She wants to be cruel ↓ woman-like*

*She had a kid?*

*nature vs. Supernature*

31

When Macbeth arrives, Lady Macbeth urges him to hide his true feelings and leave everything to her.

**51**    **keen** sharp

**55**    **Greater ... hereafter** greater still by the royal greeting that will be yours in the future

**57**    **ignorant present** i.e. the present does not know what the future will be

**58**    **The future ... instant** a projection of the future in this very moment

**60**    **as he purposes** that is his intention

**60–1**  **O never ... see** The sun will not be shining on Duncan tomorrow

**62–3**  **Your face ... matters** People who look at you will feel that something is wrong

**63–4**  **To beguile ... time** To deceive the world your face must express what is going on around you

**64–5**  **bear ... tongue** your look, your hand, your speech must all express welcome

**66–8**  **He that's ... dispatch** As Lady Macbeth speaks of Duncan's arrival she uses three phrases: 'provided for', 'great business', 'my dispatch' which are all a **play on words** (see Glossary p. 242) relating to the planned murder.

**69–70** **Which ... masterdom** which (the 'great business') will absolutely ensure our royal future and control

**71–2**  **Only ... fear** Just look people straight in the eye; if you keep on changing your expression, people with know you're afraid

That my keen knife see not the wound it makes,
Nor heaven peep through the blanket of the dark,
To cry 'Hold, hold!'

*Macbeth is a dark character.*

*Enter* MACBETH

*First words to him*

Great Glamis, worthy Cawdor,
Greater than both, by the all-hail hereafter,
Thy letters have transported me beyond
This ignorant present, and I feel now
The future in the instant.

*Lives in the future hoping to be king queen*

MACBETH                     My dearest love.
Duncan comes here tonight.

*FOCUS on death of Duncan*

L. MACBETH                  And when goes hence?

MACBETH     Tomorrow, as he purposes.

L. MACBETH                       O never                    60
*predictable* Shall sun that morrow see.

*FS Live psychologically in night after murder*

Your face, my Thane, is as a book where men
May read strange matters. To beguile the time,
Look like the time; bear welcome in your eye,
Your hand, your tongue look like th' innocent
   flower,                                        *Hide the truth*  65
   *devil*
But be the serpent under't. He that's coming
Must be provided for; and you shall put
*Contrast underlines why it isn't correct to kill* This night's great business into my dispatch,
Which shall to all our nights and days to come
Give solely sovereign sway and masterdom.      70

MACBETH    We will speak further.   *Hesitant.*

L. MACBETH                  Only look up clear;
To alter favour ever is to fear.
Leave all the rest to me.

*In control*                        [*Exeunt*

*she'll be in control until Banquo dies*

*· They both know they'll kill the king*

33

The king and his retinue arrive at Inverness, and Duncan is greeted warmly by Lady Macbeth.

| | |
|---|---|
| **1** | **pleasant seat** agreeable situation: an example of **dramatic irony** (see Glossary p. 239). |
| **1–3** | **The air ... senses** We find the light and sweet air gently relaxing |
| **3** | **guest of summer** (see next line) The house martin is a summer visitor. |
| **4** | **temple-haunting martlet** house martin (a bird similar to a swallow); Banquo claims to have seen the bird near churches. |
| **5** | **mansionry** nest-building |
| **6–8** | **No jutty ... cradle** There is no projection, frieze, buttress or useful spot where it will not build its nest, which seems to hang, and is the cradle to contain its young |
| **8–9** | **Where ... delicate** I have always noticed that where they fly and breed the air is sweet |
| **11** | **The love ... trouble** Sometimes the affection which surrounds us can be tiresome |
| **12** | **Which ... love** but as it is love we are still glad of it |
| **12–14** | **Herein ... your trouble** By saying this I am showing you how you should ask God to reward us for being a nuisance to you and thank us for the trouble we cause |
| **14–15** | **All ... double** Everything we do for you is done twice and then doubly checked |
| **16–17** | **Were ... against** it would be pathetic and feeble business to compare with |
| **18** | **our house** our family |
| | **those of old** former honours |
| **19** | **late ... up to** recent honours on top of |
| **20** | **hermits** People who pray for the souls of benefactors. |
| **21** | **coursed** chased |

## Scene 6

*Oboes and torches*

*Enter* DUNCAN, MALCOLM, DONALBAIN, BANQUO, LENNOX,
MACDUFF, ROSS, ANGUS, *and attendants*

*[handwritten: nemesis]*

DUNCAN   This castle hath a pleasant seat. The air   *[handwritten: Dramatic Irony]*
Nimbly and sweetly recommends itself   *[handwritten: we know it won't]*
Unto our gentle senses.   *[handwritten: be pleasant]*

BANQUO   *[handwritten: Build nests]*   This guest of summer,
The temple-haunting martlet does approve,
By his loved mansionry, that the heaven's breath   5
Smells wooingly here. No jutty, frieze,
Buttress, nor coign of vantage, but this bird   *[handwritten: nests everywhere]*
Hath made his pendent bed and procreant cradle.
*[handwritten: They don't know]* Where they most breed and haunt, I have
      observed
The air is delicate.

*Enter* LADY MACBETH

DUNCAN                    See, see our honoured hostess!   10
The love that follows us sometime is our trouble,
Which still we thank as love. Herein I teach you,
How you shall bid God 'ield us for your pains,
And thank us for your trouble.   *[handwritten: very grateful for manipulation]*

L. MACBETH                    All our service
In every point twice done, and then done double,   15
Were poor and single business to contend
Against those honours deep and broad wherewith
Your Majesty loads our house. For those of old,
And the late dignities heaped up to them,
We rest your hermits.

DUNCAN                    Where's the Thane of Cawdor?   20
We coursed him at the heels, and had a purpose
*[handwritten: They can catch up]*

Duncan is full of compliments for Macbeth and Lady Macbeth.

**22**  **purveyor** A steward who would go ahead to organise things for royal visits.

**23**  **holp** helped

**25–8**  **Your servants ... your own** Your subjects are always ready to give you your due; your subjects always have their servants, themselves and everything they own ready to be accounted for, so that when the king wishes to check he can claim what is his

Outside the banqueting hall, Macbeth thinks over the decision to murder Duncan.

**SD**  *sewer* master of ceremonies

**1–2**  **If it ... quickly** If it ended once the murder is committed, then it would be good to get it over with quickly

**3**  **trammel** catch, gather up

**4**  **his surcease** Duncan's death

  **success** 1) a good result 2) succession to the throne

**6**  **here** in this world

  **bank and shoal** sandbank and shallows

**7**  **jump** risk

  **the life to come** what happens in the life after death

  **these cases** (of murder)

**8**  **have judgement here** are sentenced on earth

**8–9**  **but ... instructions** have lessons in bloodshed

**9–10**  **return ... inventor** rebound on the person who started it

**11**  **Commends** recommends

  **ingredience** ingredients, contents

**12**  **He's ... trust** He has two reasons to be confident in his safety here

**13**  **First ... kinsman** firstly, not only am I his relative

*wanted to tell L. Macbeth*

To be his purveyor; but he rides well,
And his great love, sharp as his spur, hath holp him
To his home before us. Fair and noble hostess,
We are your guest tonight.

L. MACBETH                    Your servants ever          25
Have theirs, themselves, and what is theirs, in count,
To make their audit at your Highness' pleasure,
Still to return your own.

DUNCAN                    Give me your hand. *Macbeth is*
Conduct me to mine host, (we love him highly,) *still loved.*
And shall continue our graces towards him.          30
By your leave, hostess.

                              [*Exeunt*

## Scene ❼

*Oboes and torches*

*Enter a sewer, and divers servants with dishes
and service, and pass over the stage. Then enter*
MACBETH

*It will never end → ~~Get~~ guilt.*

MACBETH ( If it were done, when 'tis done, then 'twere well
*⅃ Genuine* It were done quickly.) If th' assassination
*thoughts* Could trammel up the consequence, and catch
*↓* (With his surcease success:) that but this blow *Simple idea*
*to himself* Might be the be-all and the end-all here,          5
But here, upon this bank and shoal of time,
*He'd risk* (We'd jump the life to come.) But in these cases *Judged in life &*
*his* (We still have judgement here,) that we but teach *afterlife*
*afterlife* Bloody instructions, which, being taught, return
*↓* To plague th' inventor. This even-handed justice          10
*go to hell* Commends th' ingredience of our poisoned
                    chalice
To our own lips. He's here in double trust: *Thinks of all the*
First, as (I am his kinsman) and his subject, *consequences.*
                    *Family*
· *First he decides he won't kill Duncan*

**37**

By the time that Lady Macbeth comes to find him, Macbeth has changed his mind. The murder will not go ahead. Lady Macbeth is scornful of her husband. She accuses him of cowardice and a lack of love for her.

**14**   **Strong both** both of these already strong reasons

**17**   **Hath borne ... meek** has exercised his powers so humbly

**18**   **clear** free of corruption

**20**   **deep ... taking-off** deadly sin of his murder

**21–5**   **pity ... wind** Duncan's innocence and virtue will cut through the storm of horror, and angels riding on the wind will let everybody know about this murder so that tears of pity will fall like rain

**25–7**   **I have ... ambition** The only thing which spurs me on is ambition

**27**   **Vaulting** prepared to go out of turn, leap over others in line

      **o'erleaps** vaults too far

**28**   **th' other** the other side

**34**   **would be** ought to be

**34–5**   **worn now ... so soon** enjoyed whilst they are at their best, and not put away

**36**   **dressed** Part of the continuing **metaphor** (see Glossary p. 241) that honours, and his hope, are like clothes that you enjoy wearing when they are new and bright.

**36–8**   **Hath it ... freely?** Has it been asleep and woken up the day after with a hangover, regretting what it said so carelessly when it was drunk?

**39**   **Such ... love** I consider your love worthless as a drunken promise

**39–41**   **Art thou ... desire?** Are you afraid to carry out the deed with the same bravery that you show in your longing for it?

**41**   **that** the crown

**42**   **thou esteem'st** you regard

      **the ornament of life** (also the crown)

**43**   **live ... esteem** spend your life considering yourself a coward

Strong both against the deed; then, as his host,
Who should against his murderer shut the door,          15
Not bear the knife myself. Besides, this Duncan
Hath borne his faculties so meek, hath been
So clear in his great office, that his virtues
Will plead like angels, trumpet-tongued, against
The deep damnation of his taking-off,                  20
And pity, like a naked new-born babe,
Striding the blast, or heaven's cherubin, horsèd
Upon the sightless couriers of the air,
Shall blow the horrid deed in every eye,
That tears shall drown the wind. I have no spur        25
To prick the sides of my intent, but only
Vaulting ambition, which o'erleaps itself,
And falls on th' other –

*(Enter* LADY MACBETH*)*

                              How now? What news?

L. MACBETH  He has almost supped. Why have you left the chamber?

MACBETH  Hath he asked for me?

L. MACBETH                    Know you not he has?         30

MACBETH  We will proceed no further in this business.
He hath honoured me of late, and I have bought
Golden opinions from all sorts of people,
Which would be worn now in their newest gloss,
Not cast aside so soon.

L. MACBETH                  Was the hope drunk,           35
Wherein you dressed yourself? Hath it slept since?
And wakes it now to look so green and pale
At what it did so freely? From this time
Such I account thy love. Art thou afeard
To be the same in thine own act and valour              40
As thou art in desire? Wouldst thou have that
Which thou esteem'st the ornament of life,
And live a coward in thine own esteem,

**Handwritten annotations:** He's the host. He jumps. His ambition will put his life in danger. retribution / Duncan is associated with life. motivation ambition. They have a plan. Blame him for not being decisive. You don't love me. coward. You promised. He's not brave enough.

When Macbeth begins to waver, Lady Macbeth explains her plan. Macbeth is impressed both by his wife's plan, and by her attitude.

44      **Letting ... 'I would'** letting fear get the better of desire

45      **adage** A **proverb** (see Glossary p. 242) – the cat wanted to catch fish without getting her paws wet.

46      **I dare ... man** I dare to do everything fitting for a man to do

47      **Who ... none** A man who dares to do more is no man at all (Macbeth is saying that to kill a king is not a fitting enterprise for a man.)

48      **break this enterprise** suggest this plan

49      **durst** dared to

50      **to be more ... were** to become king

51–2      **Nor time ... adhere** Neither the time nor the place was convenient then

52      **would make both** were determined to make both fit

53–4      **that ... unmake you** time and place are here now, and you are incapable

54      **I have given suck** I have fed a child at my breast

58–9      **had I ... this** if I had sworn to such an undertaking as you have done in this case

59      **We fail?** Lady Macbeth either suggests that failure is impossible – or, if the question mark has been mistaken for an exclamation mark, she would be saying 'Well, that would be that'.

60      **But ... sticking-place** Only wind up your courage to its tightest point

64–7      **with wine ... only** They will be so drunk that they will remember nothing.

68      **drenchèd** drowned

70–1      **What not ... officers** We can blame the drunken guards

72      **quell** slaughter

72–4      **Bring ... males** You should produce male children only

73      **undaunted mettle** determined spirit

Letting 'I dare not' wait upon 'I would,'
Like the poor cat i' th' adage? *[compared to a cat]* *[pussy]*

MACBETH                                        Prithee peace.                    45

I dare do all that may become a man;
Who dares do more is none.  *[no man could do more.]*

L. MACBETH                        What beast was't then,
That made you break this enterprise to me?  *[you promised.]*
When you durst do it, then you were a man;  *[not anymore.]*
*[Tempting him with]* And to be more than what you were, you would        50
*[his ambition.]* Be so much more the man. Nor time nor place
Did then adhere, and yet you would make both.
They have made themselves, and that their fitness

*[now]* *[not make]*
*[similar to unsex]* Does unmake you. I have given suck, and know
*[She's more of a man than he is.]* How tender 'tis to love the babe that milks me –        55
*[she had a child.]* I would while it was smiling in my face
Have plucked my nipple from his boneless gums,
*[comparison to show her worst thoughts.]* And dashed the brains out, had I so sworn
As you have done to this.

MACBETH                        If we should fail?

L. MACBETH                        We fail?

But screw your courage to the sticking-place,        60
*[Explain how it's supposed to happen]* And we'll not fail. When Duncan is asleep -
Whereto the rather shall his day's hard journey
Soundly invite him – his two chamberlains    *[Macbeth kills Duncan]*
Will I with wine and wassail so convince,
That memory, the warder of the brain,        *[L. Mb drunks them]*
*[drunk]* Shall be a fume, and the receipt of reason        65
A limbeck only. When in swinish sleep        *[Blame murder on them.]*
Their drenchèd natures lie as in a death,
What cannot you and I perform upon
Th' unguarded Duncan? What not put upon        70
His spongy officers, who shall bear the guilt
Of our great quell?        *[needs children.]*  *[Importance of children]*

MACBETH                ( Bring forth men-children only,)
For thy undaunted mettle should compose
                *[He's thinking ahead]*

41

Macbeth is determined to carry out the murder.

**74**      **received** accepted as true, assumed

**77**      **Who ... other** Who would dare to make anything else of it?

**78**      **we shall ... roar** we shall be loud in our sorrow and anger

**79**      **bend up** make taut like a bow, i.e. make ready

**80**      **Each corporal agent** every power in my body

**81**      **mock the time** deceive the world

*masculine & strong → L. MB*

(Nothing but males.) Will it not be received,
When we have marked with blood those sleepy
  *two   use their daggers → Frame the guards.*
Of his own chamber, and used their very daggers,
That they have done't?

L. MACBETH                             Who dares receive it other,
As we shall make our griefs and clamour roar
Upon his death?

MACBETH                    (I am settled,) and bend up
Each corporal agent to this terrible feat.                    80
Away, and mock the time with fairest show:
(False face must hide what the false heart doth
   know.)          *makes his mind up.* [*Exeunt*

*quote*
  ↳ *Hide reality*
    *relate to p. 33*

# Act 1 scenes 4 to 7

## Character: Lady Macbeth

Scene 5 is the first time we meet Macbeth's wife. After she has read his letter telling her the news, she speaks about his character. She sees that her husband has the ambition to be King, but does he have what it takes? She lists her doubts.

**Work on your own**

1   Read scene 5 lines 15–30 again.

2   Make a list of the reasons why Lady Macbeth questions her husband's character. For each reason, find a quotation backing it up, and explain why this supports the point you have made. Use a table like the one below. It has been started for you.

| Point | Evidence | Explanation |
|-------|----------|-------------|
| He is not ruthless enough. | His nature is 'too full o' th' milk of human kindness \| To catch the nearest way'. | He is too kind and gentle to do what is required. |
|  |  |  |

**Work with a partner**

3   Share your ideas.

4   Think about what this scene tells us about Lady Macbeth herself. Read again lines 38–54.

5   Look at this list of qualities:

ambitious   clear-sighted   cruel   determined   domineering
dynamic   intelligent   loving   unnatural   wicked

Which do you think is the best to describe Lady Macbeth, and which is the worst? Write them all down in order of suitability, with the best at the top and the worst at the bottom.

6   Now write your top four qualities into a Point, Evidence, Explanation table like the one above.

# Performance: Macbeth and Lady Macbeth

**Work with a partner**

1  Read silently Act 1 scene 7 from line 28 (Macbeth: How now? What news?) to line 72 (Macbeth: Bring forth men-children only).

2  If you were rehearsing these lines, you could perform them in different ways. For example:

   **A**  When Lady Macbeth enters, Macbeth has decided that he definitely will not go any further with their plan. He is absolutely determined about this. Lady Macbeth was expecting this and pretends to be furious with him, just to make him change his mind.

   **B**  When Lady Macbeth enters, Macbeth still hasn't made up his mind. He is completely unsure of himself. Lady Macbeth is genuinely amazed at this and has to work hard to persuade him to continue with what they had planned.

   Work on option 'A'. Each take a part. For your character, think about:
   - how you will speak
   - your facial expressions
   - your movements
   - your gestures.

3  Rehearse the scene.

4  Now do the same for option 'B'.

5  Discuss the two versions.

   **a**  Which seemed the more convincing and why?

   **b**  Can you think of any other ways in which these lines might be performed?

## *Follow-up*

**Work with a partner**

1  Read Act 1 scene 5 lines 58–73.

2  Discuss two alternative ways of performing these lines.

3  Follow the same pattern as above to rehearse each interpretation.

45

# Macbeth's mood

In Act 1 scene 7, Macbeth's mood changes as the scene progresses. At the beginning of the scene he expresses his doubts about what he and his wife are planning to do. By the end of the scene Lady Macbeth has told him to 'screw your courage to the sticking-place' and he is ready to go ahead with the plan.

You can use a graph to plot Macbeth's doubts and determination as the scene progresses:

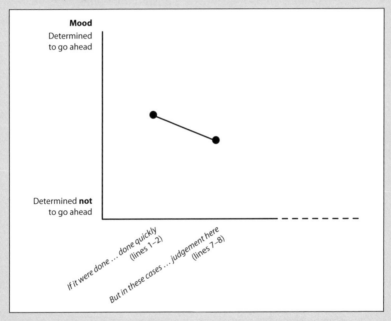

**Work with a partner**

1  On a large sheet of paper draw the chart above.

2  Pick out the moments in the scene when Macbeth's mood seems to change.

3  Mark each one on the chart. Write the relevant lines below, including the line numbers.

**Work in a group of four**

4  Share and discuss your charts.

46

# Plot summary quiz

The 12 short quotations below sum up the story of scenes 4 to 7.

1  Work out the correct order for them.

2  Work out who said each one.

**A**

Fair and noble hostess,
We are your guest tonight.

**B**

False face must hide what the false heart doth know.

**C**

He that's coming
Must be provided for…

**D**

If it were done, when 'tis done, then 'twere well
It were done quickly.

**E**

If we should fail?

**F**

Is execution done on Cawdor?

**G**

The raven himself is hoarse
That croaks the fatal entrance of Duncan
Under my battlements.

**H**

This castle hath a pleasant seat…

**I**

Thou wouldst be great,
Art not without ambition, but without
The illness should attend it.

**J**

…We will establish our estate upon
Our eldest, Malcolm…

**K**

We will proceed no further
in this business.

**L**

Your face, my Thane, is as a book where men
May read strange matters.

47

Banquo and his son, Fleance, are on their way to bed having just left Duncan. They meet Macbeth, and Banquo mentions that he has had dreams about the three witches.

1    **How ... night** What time is it?

2    **is down** has set

4    **husbandry** thrift, economy

5    **Their candles ... out** it is a night without stars

     **that too** (possibly a sword–belt or a cloak)

6    **heavy summons** deep tiredness

7    **would not** do not want to

7–9  **Merciful ... repose** I pray you, angels who drive away evil spirits, do away with my nightmares

13   **unusual pleasure** particularly good humour

14   **largesse** gifts (usually of money)

     **your offices** those who run your household

15   **This diamond ... withal** In addition he greets your wife with this diamond

16   **shut up** has gone to bed

17–19 **Being ... wrought** Because we were unprepared, our wish to entertain freely was limited

# Act Two

## Scene ❶

*Enter* BANQUO, *and* FLEANCE *bearing a torch before him*

<u>remind audience it's night.</u>

BANQUO    How goes the night, boy? <u>IT'S NIGHT.</u>

FLEANCE   The moon is down. I have not heard the clock.

BANQUO    And she goes down at twelve.

FLEANCE                               I take't, 'tis later, sir.

BANQUO    Hold, take my sword. There's husbandry in heaven,

<u>Very dark</u> Their candles are all out. Take thee that too.                    5

A heavy summons lies like lead upon me,

*Thinks of what he's been promised.* (And yet I would not sleep) Merciful powers,

Restrain in me the cursed thoughts that nature

Gives way to in repose.   <u>Tempted but doesn't give in</u>
                                      <u>∟ not Macbeth.</u>

*Enter* MACBETH, *and a servant with a torch*

                          ( Give me my sword.) <u>foreshadow</u>

Who's there?                  <u>Lack of trust</u>                    10

MACBETH   A friend. ) <u>for now</u>

BANQUO    What sir, not yet at rest? The King's a-bed.

He hath been in unusual pleasure, and

Sent forth great largesse to your offices.

This diamond he greets your wife withal,                          15

By the name of most kind hostess, and shut up

In measureless content.

MACBETH                          Being unprepared,

Our will became the servant to defect,

Which else should free have wrought.

BANQUO                                         All's well,

( I dreamt last night of the three weird sisters.)               20

                    <u>wants to talk</u>

49

Macbeth hints that he looks for Banquo's support in future, but Banquo makes it clear that he will only act honourably. Macbeth, when he is alone, imagines that he sees a dagger, leading him to Duncan's room.

**22**      **entreat … serve** find a convenient time

**23**      **We would spend** we should spend

**24**      **At … leisure** When you may have the time which suits

**25**      **If you … 'tis** 1) If you follow my advice when we talk 2) If you will support me when the time comes; a double meaning which may also include the suggestion, 'When I am king'.

**26**      **honour** rewards

        **So I … none** As long as I don't lose any

**27**      **augment it** gain higher status

**27–9**    **still … counselled** if I can keep my heart free from guilt and my loyalty unquestioned then I shall listen to you

**35–7**    **I have … sight?** I cannot take hold of you and yet you are still visible. Are you not, deadly vision, capable of being grasped physically as you are by sight?

**39**      **heat-oppressed** feverish

**40**      **yet** still

        **palpable** capable of being touched

**41**      **As this … draw** as my own dagger which I'm unsheathing now

**42**      **Thou marshall'st … going** You are leading me in the direction I was going

**44–5**    **Mine eyes … rest** My eyes deceive me if the other senses are right, or else they are correct and more reliable than all the other senses

**46**      **dudgeon** hilt

        **gouts** drops

**47**      **There's no such thing** It doesn't exist

To you they have showed some truth.

MACBETH                                   I think not of them. *lies*

*talk later* {
Yet when we can entreat an hour to serve,
We would spend it in some words upon that
    business,
}

If you would grant the time.

BANQUO                                   At your kind'st leisure.

MACBETH    If you shall cleave to my consent, when 'tis,               25
It shall make honour for you. *subtle trying to convin* Banquo

BANQUO                                   So I lose none
In seeking to augment it, but still keep
My bosom franchised, and allegiance clear,
I shall be counselled.

MACBETH                                   Good repose the while.

BANQUO    Thanks sir. The like to you.                                30

[*Exeunt* BANQUO *and* FLEANCE

MACBETH    Go bid thy mistress, when my drink is ready,
She strike upon the bell. Get thee to bed.

*killing signal*

[*Exit servant*

*Supernatural*
*In his head*
Is this a dagger which I see before me, *Apparition*
The handle toward my hand? Come, let me clutch *Invisible dagger*
    thee.                        *He's a murderer*
I have thee not, and yet I see thee still.                             35
Art thou not, fatal vision, sensible
To feeling as to sight? Or art thou but          *Is this real life*
A dagger of the mind, a false creation,          *or is It fanta sea*
Proceeding from the heat-oppressed brain? *guilt*
I see thee yet, in form as palpable                                   40
As this which now I draw. *encouraged him to get a*
Thou marshall'st me the way that I was going, *dagger.*
And such an instrument I was to use.
Mine eyes are made the fools o' th' other senses,
Or else worth all the rest. I see thee still;                         45
And on thy blade and dudgeon gouts of blood,
Which was not so before. There's no such thing.

*leads to murder.*

Macbeth's mind is in turmoil. He hears the bell – a signal arranged with Lady Macbeth – and he goes to commit the murder of Duncan.

**48–9**   **It is ... eyes** Thoughts of murder are playing tricks with my eyes

**49**   **the one half-world** our hemisphere

**50–1**   **Nature ... sleep** the world sleeps and nightmares abound

**51**   **curtained sleep** 1) curtains round a bed 2) eyelids

**52**   **Hecate** The goddess of witchcraft (pronounced 'Hecket', with the stress on the first syllable).

   **offerings** rituals

**52–4**   **withered ... watch** shrivelled murder, roused to action by the wolf on guard, whose howl is his watchman

**54–6**   **thus ... ghost** moves swiftly and quietly, much as Tarquin did, like a ghost towards the intended act

**55**   **Tarquin** In 509 BC, Tarquin, son of the king of Rome, raped his hostess, Lucretia, in the dead of night.

**58**   **prate ... whereabout** prattle about, tell where I am

**59–60**   **And take ... with it** and remove the horror by breaking the silence and the tension

**60–1**   **Whiles ... gives** As long as I continue to anticipate the deed he remains alive. Talking too much will cool the enthusiasm to act

Lady Macbeth has made the preparations for murder, and she awaits her husband's return.

**2**   **What ... fire** What has snuffed them out has fired me up

   **quenched** 1) satisfied their thirst 2) put out, extinguished (an **extended image** – see Glossary p. 240)

**4**   **stern'st** cruellest

**5**   **surfeited grooms** drunken servants

**6**   **mock their charge** make a mockery of their duty

   **possets** A posset was a hot milk drink with added liquor.

**7–8**   **That death ... die** they are on the borders of life and death as death and their natural powers battle over them

(It is the bloody business which informs
Thus to mine eyes) Now o'er the one half-world

*Dark*
*Supernature*

Nature seems dead, and wicked dreams abuse          50
The curtained sleep. Witchcraft celebrates
Pale Hecate's offerings, and withered murder,
Alarumed by his sentinel the wolf,
Whose howl's his watch, thus with his stealthy pace,
With Tarquin's ravishing strides, towards his design  55
Moves like a ghost. Thou sure and firm-set earth,

*He's*
*guilty*

Hear not my steps, which way they walk, for fear
Thy very stones prate of my whereabout,
And take the present horror from the time,   *He's still alive*
Which now suits with it. (Whiles I threat, he lives.)   60
Words to the heat of deeds too cold breath gives.

                    *He wants to act quickly*
                                    *[A bell rings*

*Bell and*
*dagger*
*invite him*

I go, and it is done. (The bell invites me.)   *Signal*
Hear it not Duncan, for it is a knell –
That summons thee to heaven or to hell. – *rhyme*

                                        (*[Exit*

                                        *Decision.*

## Scene ❷

*Enter* LADY MACBETH

L. MACBETH  That which hath made them drunk hath made me
            bold.  *alcohol & ambition*
            What hath quenched them hath (given me fire.) *Decisive*
            Hark! Peace!  *nightly critter → supernatural.*
            It was the (owl that shrieked,) the fatal bellman,   *Macbeth*
            Which gives the stern'st good night. (He is about it.) *killing Duncan.*

*Imagines*
*to explain*
*to the*
*audience.*

            The doors are open, and the surfeited grooms          5
            Do mock their charge with snores. I have drugged
              their possets,
            That death and nature do contend about them,
            Whether they live or die.

              *murder  happened*

Macbeth enters, distracted and nervous. He has committed the murder and is obsessed with thoughts of damnation.

| | | |
|---|---|---|
| **10** | **'tis not done** | he hasn't managed to do it |

**10–11** **Th' attempt ... us** If he has tried to kill Duncan and not carried it out then we are ruined

**12** **resembled** looked like

**13** **I had done't** I would have done it

**18** **sorry** wretched

**20** **one** the other one who shared the room with Donalbain (we do not know who)

**22** **addressed them** prepared themselves

**25** **hangman's** executioner's

**26** **Listening** Hearing

**28** **Consider ... deeply** You are reading too much into this

MACBETH    [*Within*]          Who's there? <u>What ho!</u>

L. MACBETH   Alack, I am afraid they have awaked,

*Snort*          And 'tis not done. Th' attempt and not the deed    10

*sentences*     Confounds us. Hark! I laid their daggers ready;

*nerves*       He could not miss 'em. Had he not resembled

My father as he slept, I had done't. *Associated with*

*Enter* MACBETH    *guilt builds up    Family*

                                    My husband!

MACBETH    I have done the deed. Didst thou not hear a noise?

L. MACBETH   I heard the owl scream and the crickets cry.    15

Did not you speak?    *night*

MACBETH               When?

L. MACBETH                  Now.

MACBETH                      As I descended?

L. MACBETH   Ay.

MACBETH       Hark! Who lies i' th' second chamber?

L. MACBETH                          Donalbain.

MACBETH    This is a sorry sight. [*Looks on his hands*

L. MACBETH   A foolish thought, to say a sorry sight.

MACBETH    <u>There's one did laugh in's sleep, and one cried</u>

      'Murder!'    *Duncan's* <u>sons</u>    20

That they did wake each other. I stood and heard

them.

But they did say their prayers, and addressed them

Again to sleep.

L. MACBETH             There are two lodged together.

MACBETH    One cried 'God bless us!' and 'Amen!' the other,

As they had seen me with these hangman's hands.   25

Listening their fear, <u>I could not say 'Amen',</u>   *going*

<u>When they did say 'God bless us!'</u>    *to hell*

L. MACBETH   Consider it not so deeply.

MACBETH    But wherefore could not I pronounce 'Amen'?

Lady Macbeth tells Macbeth to pull himself together. He has brought the daggers away from the murder scene and refuses to take them back. Lady Macbeth takes them. There is a knocking at the castle gate.

**31–2**   **These deeds ... mad** You must not think like this about what we have done. Such thoughts will drive us mad

**33**   **Methought** I thought

**35**   **sleave of care** 1) sleeve 2) skein of silk; the **imagery** (see Glossary p. 240) suggests making good a worn piece of knitting. Sleep 'mends' distress.

**36–8**   **The death ... feast** the end of every day, the warm bath after hard work, healing for hurt minds, in short the second main course offered at life's feast (The imagery of the comfort that sleep can bring continues.)

**43**   **unbend** slacken, undermine

**44**   **so brainsickly** with such a sick mind

**45**   **witness** evidence

**50**   **Infirm of purpose!** Weak-minded man!

**52**   **but as pictures** only representations of the living person

      **the eye of childhood** a child's eyes

**53**   **painted devil** picture of the devil

      **painted** coloured

**54**   **gild ... grooms** smear his blood on the grooms' faces

**55**   **guilt** This word picks up the word 'gild' making a **play on words** (see Glossary p. 242).

I had most need of blessing, and 'Amen'          30
Stuck in my throat.   *worried.*

L. MACBETH                    These deeds must not be thought
After these ways; so, it will make us mad. *) FS*

MACBETH  Methought I heard a voice cry 'Sleep no more! *They're*
Macbeth does murder sleep' – the innocent sleep, *haunted by guilt.*
Sleep that knits up the ravelled sleave of care,          35
The death of each day's life, sore labour's bath,
Balm of hurt minds, great nature's second course,
Chief nourisher in life's feast. *need sleep to cure mind*

L. MACBETH                    What do you mean?

MACBETH  Still it cried 'Sleep no more!' to all the house,
'Glamis hath murdered sleep, and therefore
    Cawdor   *from the first moment he's been guilty*          40
Shall sleep no more, Macbeth shall sleep no more.'

L. MACBETH  Who was it that thus cried? Why, worthy Thane,
*caring*      You do unbend your noble strength, to think
So brainsickly of things. (Go get some water,
And wash this filthy witness from your hand.)          45
Why did you bring these daggers from the place?
They must lie there. Go carry them, and smear
The sleepy grooms with blood.   *Frame them*

MACBETH                                        I'll go no more.
I am afraid to think what I have done.
Look on't again I dare not. ) *not afraid to admit guilt.*

L. MACBETH        *she's scared too*   (Infirm of purpose!)          50
*wants to appear strong*  Give me the daggers. The sleeping and the dead
Are but as pictures. 'Tis the eye of childhood
That fears a painted devil. If he do bleed,
I'll gild the faces of the grooms withal,
*cover in blood*  For it must seem their guilt.   [*Exit. Knock within*

MACBETH                          Whence is that knocking?  55
How is't with me, when every noise appals me?
(What hands are here?) Ha! They pluck out mine eyes.

*( Duncan's blood is valuable like gold.*
*Doesn't recognize his hands*

57

Lady Macbeth returns with blood-stained hands. The knocking at the gate continues and they hurry to put on nightclothes.

**58**       **Neptune** Roman god of the sea.

**60**       **incarnadine** dye blood-red

**61**       **Making ... red** turning the green ocean red

**64**       **entry** gate

             **Retire we** Let us go

**66–7**     **Your constancy ... unattended** Your self-control has deserted you

**68**       **lest ... us** in case we are needed

**69**       **show ... watchers** we are seen to be still awake

**70**       **poorly** dejectedly

**71**       **To know ... myself** I had rather be lost in thought than face the reality of my crime

**72**       **I would thou couldst** If only you could

*Sea – Holy image – Side of ocean*

*All water in the sea can't wash his hands*

Will all great Neptune's ocean wash this blood
Clean from my hand? No, this my hand will rather
The multitudinous seas incarnadine,                          60
Making the green one red.

*Enter* LADY MACBETH

L. MACBETH My hands are of your colour; but I shame
To wear a heart so white. [*Knock within*] I hear a
knocking
At the south entry. Retire we to our chamber.
A little water clears us of this deed.                        65
How easy is it then! Your constancy
Hath left you unattended. [*Knock within*] Hark,
more knocking.
Get on your nightgown, lest occasion call us,
And show us to be watchers. Be not lost
So poorly in your thoughts.                                   70

*Strong woman supports Macbeth.*

*guilty but strong.*

*contrast*

MACBETH To know my deed, 'twere best not know myself.
[*Knock within*
Wake Duncan with thy knocking. I would thou
couldst.                        [*Exeunt*

*Hates himself.*

*wish he was alive*

*He'll envy him soon*

# Act 2 scenes 1 and 2

## 'Is this a dagger which I see before me?'

This is one of Shakespeare's most famous lines. It comes at the beginning of a powerful and dramatic **soliloquy**. So how should the speech be performed?

**Work on your own**

1   Read Act 2 scene 1 lines 33–61 again. As you read, write down any pictures that come into your mind:

> lines
> 33–4    a dagger moving towards him, handle first
> 34–5

**Work with a partner**

2   You have now explored the images in the speech, but how can an actor communicate these pictures to the audience? Look again at lines 33–41 and think about these questions:

   a   Are there any clues about Macbeth's movements and actions?

   b   Are there any clues about how he should speak: fast or slow? Loud or soft? Fluently, or with hesitations?

   c   Which of these adjectives would you choose to describe his mood?

   puzzled    fearful    angry    horrified    thoughtful

   d   Can you add any adjectives of your own?

3   Now work together to produce a set of detailed guidelines for the actor playing the part of Macbeth. Write a set of bullet points explaining how you think the speech should be performed.

## *Extension*

How would you film this speech? Here are two possible approaches. Think about them and then decide how you would tackle the speech.

A   The camera stays close up on Macbeth's face for the whole speech. We hear the speech as a voiceover. We see his thoughts and feelings only in his facial expressions.

**B**  We see the actor beginning to speak the lines, then the picture dissolves into a series of 'nightmare' pictures of the knife he is describing.

# Character: Macbeth and Lady Macbeth

Scene 2 gives us a good opportunity to compare the characters of Macbeth and Lady Macbeth. At a moment of high tension, they react in contrasting ways to the murder of Duncan. For example, when Macbeth looks at his hand covered with blood, he says, 'This is a sorry sight', to which his wife replies, 'A foolish thought, to say a sorry sight.' As you look through the scene you will find many other occasions where they react in very different ways.

**Work with a partner**

1  Choose one character each. Look at your character's list below and choose four adjectives that you think best describe your character's behaviour in this scene. If you like you can combine words from the list with words you have thought of yourself.

| Macbeth | | Lady Macbeth | |
|---------|---------|-------------|---------|
| timid | fearful | soothing | calm |
| wondering | surprised | practical | irritated |
| horrified | disbelieving | down-to-earth | thoughtful |
| dithering | cowardly | scheming | clever |

2  Now copy and complete a Point Evidence Explanation table for each character. Write the chosen words in the first column and then complete the evidence and explanation for each word:

| Point | Evidence | Explanation |
|-------|----------|-------------|
| Fearful | 'I'll go no more. I am afraid to think what I have done.' | He is too frightened to go back to the murder room to replace the daggers. |
|  |  |  |

3  When you have both finished, exchange tables and discuss them.

# 'Macbeth does murder sleep'

In scene 2, we see and hear Macbeth's emotional reaction to what he has done in murdering Duncan. It is a powerful scene. Shakespeare communicates the turmoil in Macbeth's mind through a series of striking images. For example, in lines 33–8, Macbeth sees sleep as if it were a person.

## Work with a partner

1 A good way of exploring your thoughts and feelings about a poetic image is to use a web diagram:

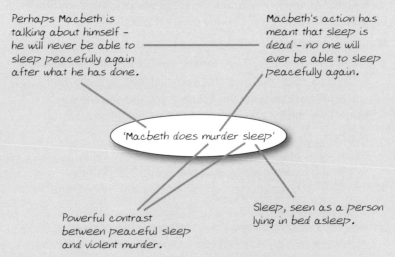

Perhaps Macbeth is talking about himself – he will never be able to sleep peacefully again after what he has done.

Macbeth's action has meant that sleep is dead – no one will ever be able to sleep peacefully again.

'Macbeth does murder sleep'

Powerful contrast between peaceful sleep and violent murder.

Sleep, seen as a person lying in bed asleep.

2 Each choose another, different image of sleep from this list:
   - 'The death of each day's life'
   - 'sore labour's bath'
   - 'Balm of hurt minds'
   - 'Chief nourisher in life's feast'

3 Each make a web diagram exploring your chosen image.

4 Exchange diagrams and see if you can suggest other ideas that your partner can add to their diagram.

# Quotation quiz

For each of these quotations, work out:

1. who said it
2. who they were speaking to
3. what it tells us about
   a. the speaker
   b. the situation
   c. any other characters.

**A**
But wherefore could not I pronounce 'Amen'?

**B**
Had he not resembled My father as he slept, I had done't.

**C**
I dreamt last night of the three Weird Sisters.

**D**
Infirm of purpose!

**E**
Is this a dagger which I see before me, The handle toward my hand?

**F**
Merciful powers, Restrain in me the cursed thoughts that nature Gives way to in repose.

**G**
Methought I heard a voice cry 'Sleep no more! Macbeth does murder sleep'…

**H**
That which hath made them drunk hath made me bold…

**I**
To know my deed, 'twere best not know myself.

**J**
Whiles I threat, he lives: Words to the heat of deeds too cold breath gives.

A porter comes to open the gate. He has been drinking and he is annoyed that his rest has been disturbed. He delays opening the gate whilst he pretends to be the porter of Hell, admitting imaginary sinners. Macduff and Lennox are at the gate.

**2**     **old** plenty of

**4**     **Beelzebub** A devil, Satan's second-in-command.

**4–5**   **Here's ... plenty** The farmer hoarded corn hoping for a poor harvest so that he would make plenty of money; when the harvest was exceptionally good, he killed himself.

**5**     **Come in time!** Come in good time, you are welcome

**6**     **have napkins ... you** bring plenty of handkerchiefs

      **enow** enough

**8**     **th' other devil's name** i.e. Satan

      **'Faith** Short for 'in faith'.

      **equivocator** double-talker (a person who uses words capable of two meanings in order to deceive)

**8–11**   **here's ... heaven** Father Garnet – also known as Farmer – was hanged in 1606 for his part in the Gunpowder Plot. At his trial he used equivocation in his defence and so all loyal subjects regarded equivocation as damnable.

**9**     **scales** (of justice)

**13–14** **here's ... French hose** It was an old joke that tailors made up customers' cloth into tight garments and kept the leftover material for themselves. 'French hose' was wide and full, and the suggestion is that the English tailor has re shaped it and stolen the extra cloth.

**15**    **roast your goose** do for you (as in the modern expression 'cook your goose'); also, heat your smoothing-iron (A tailor's iron was called a 'goose' because of the shape of the handle.)

**19–20** **primrose ... bonfire** attractive path to hell

**20**    **Anon, anon!** Just a minute!

**21**    **remember the porter** He probably hopes for a tip.

**24**    **second cock** about 3 o'clock in the morning

**27**    **Marry** Indeed

      **nose-painting** reddening of the nose

## Scene 3

*Enter a* PORTER. *Knocking within*

PORTER

*[handwritten: Satanic and equivocation]*

*[handwritten: Comic relief]*

*[handwritten: satan]*

Here's a knocking indeed! If a man were porter of hell-gate, he should have old turning the key. [*Knock within*] Knock, knock, knock. Who's there, i' th' name of Beelzebub? Here's a farmer that hanged himself on the expectation of plenty. Come in time! 5 Have napkins enow about you; here you'll sweat for't. [*Knock within*] Knock, knock. Who's there, i' th' other devil's name? 'Faith, here's an equivocator, that could swear in both the scales against either scale, who committed treason enough for God's 10 sake, yet could not equivocate to heaven. O come in, equivocator. [*Knock within*] Knock, knock, knock. Who's there? 'Faith here's an English tailor come *[handwritten: equivocation]* hither, for stealing out of a French hose. Come in tailor, here you may roast your goose. [*Knock* 15 *within*] Knock, knock. Never at quiet. What are you? But this place is too cold for hell. I'll devil-porter it no further. I had thought to have let in some of all professions, that go the primrose way to th' everlasting bonfire. [*Knock within*] Anon, anon! 20 I pray you remember the porter.    [*Opens the gate*

*[handwritten: pretends he's the gatekeeper of hell]*

*[handwritten: D.1]*

*Enter* MACDUFF *and* LENNOX

MACDUFF

Was it so late, friend, ere you went to bed,
That you do lie so late?

PORTER

*[handwritten: Ambition]*

'Faith sir, we were carousing till the second cock, and drink, sir, is a great provoker of three things. 25

MACDUFF

What three things does drink especially provoke?

PORTER

Marry sir, nose-painting, sleep, and urine. Lechery,

*[handwritten: drunk]*

*[handwritten: Lust provokes like ambition]*

Macduff and the porter indulge in banter until Macbeth arrives. Macduff
goes to wake Duncan as arranged.

**28–9**  **it provokes ... performance** it makes a man lustful but prevents
him from doing anything about it

**29–35**  **Therefore ... leaves him** Too much alcohol is a double-dealer
with lust. It creates lust in a man but hinders it; it encourages the
man and discourages him; it makes him feel ready for action but
unable to act. In the end it tricks him into sleeping and, having put
him on his back, it leaves him flat.

**35**  **giving him the lie** 1) knocking him out 2) cheating him

**36**  **gave thee the lie** held you down (like a wrestler)

**37**  **i' the ... on me** drink lay in my throat (To 'lie in one's throat'
means to tell a big lie.)

**38**  **requited** repaid

**39**  **took up my legs** 1) took my legs away (as in wrestling) 2) made
me lift up my leg (i.e. as a dog)

**40**  **made a shift** 1) managed 2) repented (put on a hair shirt, 'shift')

**cast** 1) throw 2) vomit, throw up

**45**  **timely** early

**46**  **I have ... hour** I am nearly late

**48**  **yet 'tis one** it is a trouble all the same

**The labour ... pain** A **proverb** (see Glossary p. 242) – enjoying
the work we do is the medicine for the trouble involved.

**50**  **limited service** appointed duty

**51**  **Goes ... today?** Is the king leaving today?

**did appoint so** arranged to do so

**52**  **unruly** rough

**lay** spent the night

**53**  **as they say** so they say

sir, it provokes, and unprovokes (it provokes the
desire, but it takes away the performance) Therefore
much drink may be said to be an equivocator *ambition* 30
with lechery: it makes him, and it mars him; it sets
him on, and it takes him off; it persuades him, and
disheartens him, makes him stand to, and not stand
to; in conclusion, equivocates him in a sleep, and,
giving him the lie, leaves him.                                    35

MACDUFF    I believe drink gave thee the lie last night.

PORTER     That it did, sir, i' the very throat on me; but I
           requited him for his lie, and I think, being too
           strong for him, though he took up my legs
           sometime, yet I made a shift to cast him.        40

MACDUFF    Is thy master stirring?
           (Our knocking has awaked him,) here he comes.
           *he hasn't slept*
           *Enter* MACBETH

LENNOX     Good morrow, noble sir.

MACBETH                              Good morrow, both.

MACDUFF    Is the King stirring, worthy Thane?

MACBETH                          (Not yet.) *short anxious*

MACDUFF    He did command me to call timely on him.      45
           I have almost slipped the hour.

MACBETH                              I'll bring you to him.

MACDUFF    I know this is a (joyful trouble) to you,
           But yet 'tis one. *equivocation: Duncan, witches, Macbeth*

MACBETH              (The labour we delight in physics pain.)
           This is the door.        *Hard work is good*

MACDUFF                     I'll make so bold to call,
           For 'tis my limited service.                        50

                                                   [*Exit*

LENNOX     Goes the King hence today?        *not anymore*

MACBETH                     He does — (he did appoint so.) *guilt*

LENNOX     The night has been unruly. Where we lay,
           Our chimneys were blown down, and as they say,

Lennox reports strange events in the night. Macduff returns, appalled by Duncan's death, and he tells Lennox and Macbeth to go to see for themselves. Macduff rouses the rest of the house.

**54**       **Lamentings** wailings

**56**       **dire combustion** violent commotion

**57**       **New ... time** that would happen in this unhappy time

            **obscure bird** owl (It flies at night and is rarely seen.)

**59**       **feverous ... shake** feverish and seemed to shake

**60–1**     **My young ... to it** I am not old enough to remember a night like it

**62–3**     **Tongue ... thee** Macduff is speaking in a confused way to horror (as a person). This is an example of **personification** (see Glossary p. 241).

**63**       **What's the matter?** What are you saying?

**64**       **Confusion ... masterpiece** This is the ultimate in destruction, it could not be worse

**65**       **sacrilegious** violation of what is considered sacred

            **ope** open

**65–7**     **hath broke ... building** has broken into the temple of the Lord's anointed king and stolen the life that was in that building (The king was considered to be a monarch ruling by divine right, appointed and blessed by God, so killing a king was sacrilege. The 'temple' here means the body of the king.)

**70**       **Gorgon** The female monster of Greek mythology; her hair was of writhing hissing snakes. She turned everyone who looked at her to stone.

**72**       **alarum-bell** alarm bell (the great bell of the castle)

**74**       **downy** light, of little substance

            **counterfeit** imitation

**76**       **great doom's image** picture of Judgement Day

**77**       **rise up** The dead will allegedly rise from their graves on Judgement Day.

**77**       **sprites** spirits

**78**       **countenance** face

Lamentings heard i' th' air (strange screams of death,)
And prophesying with accents terrible                            55
Of dire combustion and confused events
New hatched to the woeful time. (The obscure bird)
(Clamoured the livelong night) Some say, the earth
Was feverous, and did shake.              *Honest.*

MACBETH                                       ('Twas a rough night.)

LENNOX     My young remembrance cannot parallel               60
           A fellow to it.

           *Enter* MACDUFF

           *emotion*
MACDUFF    <u>O</u> horror, horror, horror! Tongue nor heart
           Cannot conceive nor name thee.

*lows* <u>MACBETH, LENNOX</u>  *Act like he's innocent* What's the matter?

MACDUFF    Confusion now hath made his masterpiece.   *look for*
           Most sacrilegious murder hath broke ope          65
           The Lord's anointed temple, and stole thence *information*
           The life o' th' building!

MACBETH                                    What is't you say – the life?

LENNOX     Mean you his Majesty?

MACDUFF    Approach the chamber, and destroy your sight
           With a new Gorgon. Do not bid me speak.          70
           See, and then speak yourselves.

                        [*Exeunt* MACBETH *and* LENNOX

                                    Awake, awake!
           Ring the alarum-bell! Murder and treason!
           (Banquo and Donalbain! Malcolm awake!)
           Shake off this downy sleep, death's counterfeit,
           And look on death itself! Up, up and see          75
           The great doom's image! – Malcolm! Banquo!
           As from your graves rise up, and walk like sprites,
           To countenance this horror!             [*Bell rings*

           *Enter* LADY MACBETH

L. MACBETH  What's the business,

The news of Duncan's murder is given to Banquo, Lady Macbeth, Malcolm and Donalbain. It is assumed that Duncan's guards are responsible. The circumstantial evidence suggests this.

**80**　　**trumpet ... parley** summons to meet and discuss or negotiate

**83–4**　**The repetition ... fell** if I were to tell a woman it would kill her as she heard it

**89**　　**chance** mischance, calamity

**91**　　**nothing ... mortality** human life is not important

**92**　　**toys** trifles, things of no consequence

　　　　**Renown and grace** Fame and honour

**93–4**　**The wine ... brag of** the best things in life are taken and only the dregs are left for this world to boast about

**93**　　**lees** the sediment of wine in the barrel

**94**　　**vault** 1) wine cellar 2) sky 3) burial chamber

**100**　　**badged** marked (servants wore the badge of their master)

**102**　　**distracted** perplexed, confused

That such a hideous trumpet calls to parley          80
The sleepers of the house? Speak, speak.

MACDUFF                                    (O gentle lady,)

'Tis not for you to hear what I can speak;          *not gentle.*
The repetition in a woman's ear  }  *unsexed*
Would murder as it fell.           }   *woman.*

*Enter* BANQUO          *ur next*

O Banquo, Banquo,
Our royal master's murdered.

L. MACBETH                              Woe, alas!          85
What, in our house?

BANQUO                      (Too cruel anywhere.)  *FS: he'll be*
Dear Duff, I prithee contradict thyself   *murdered*
And say it is not so.                       *somewhere else.*

*Enter* MACBETH *and* LENNOX

                                          *FS*
MACBETH      Had I but died an hour before this chance,
*He'll kill*      I had lived a blessed time; for from this instant,          90
*more*            There's nothing serious in mortality. )  *Human life is*
*people*          All is but toys. Renown and grace is dead,  *not important*
*nothing*         The wine of life is drawn, and the mere lees
*matters*         Is left this vault to brag of.          *Life is shit.*
*following*
*the murder.*  *Enter* MALCOLM *and* DONALBAIN

DONALBAIN  What is amiss?

MACBETH                      You are, and do not know it.          95
The spring, the head, the fountain of your blood  } *lineage.*
Is stopped, the very source of it is stopped.

MACDUFF      Your royal father's murdered.

MALCOLM                              O, by whom?

LENNOX       Those of his chamber, as it seemed, had done't.
Their hands and faces were all badged with blood,          100
So were their daggers, which unwiped we found
Upon their pillows. They stared, and were distracted.

Macbeth announces that he has killed the guards and says that his love for Duncan drove him to do it. Lady Macbeth collapses and is taken for treatment. Banquo begins to take charge of the situation.

**104**     **fury** frenzy

**106**     **amazed** frantic

          **temperate** level-headed

**108–9**   **The expedition ... reason** The overwhelming need to express my love was stronger than my common sense, which would have held me back

**108**     **expedition** rush

**109**     **pauser** delay (caused by reason)

**110**     **laced** decorated

**111**     **breach in nature** break in the wall of life

**112**     **ruin** death

          **wasteful** destructive

**113**     **steeped** dyed

**114**     **Unmannerly breeched** indecently clothed

          **refrain** hold himself back

**116**     **make's** make his

**117**     **Look to** Look after

**118–19**  **Why do ... ours?** Why are we silent when this matter concerns us most closely?

**120–2**   **What ... us?** What could we possibly say here, where someone could be watching us, waiting for the opportunity to do the same to us?

**121**     **auger-hole** spy-hole

**123**     **not yet brewed** not ready for pouring out yet

**124**     **Upon ... motion** ready to move

**125**     **naked frailties** Only Macduff and Lennox are properly dressed.

**128**     **Fears ... shake us** Fears and uncertainties disturb us

**130**     **undivulged pretence** hidden intentions

**131**     **treasonous malice** ill-will towards the crown

No man's life was to be trusted with them.

MACBETH   O yet I do repent me of my fury,
That I did kill them. ) *putting suspicion on him*

MACDUFF                    Wherefore did you so?   105

MACBETH   Who can be wise, amazed, temperate and furious,
*mixed* Loyal and neutral, in a moment? No man.
*emotions* The expedition of my violent love)   *Guilt.*
Outran the pauser, reason.) Here lay Duncan,
His silver skin laced with his golden blood,   110
And his gashed stabs looked like a breach in nature)
*not even* For ruin's wasteful entrance; there the murderers,
*lying, He's* Steeped in the colours of their trade, their daggers
*sad &* Unmannerly breeched with gore. Who could refrain,
*guilty.* That had a heart to love, and in that heart   115
Courage to make's love known?   *very emotional*

L. MACBETH                    Help me hence, ho!   [*Faints*

MACDUFF   Look to the lady.   *distract to protect Macbeth*

MALCOLM   [*Aside* to DONALBAIN] Why do we hold our tongues,
That most may claim this argument for ours? ) *suspicious*

DONALBAIN [*Aside* to MALCOLM] What should be spoken   120
Here where our fate, hid in an auger-hole,
May rush and seize us? Let's away; our tears
Are not yet brewed.

MALCOLM   [*Aside* to DONALBAIN] Nor our strong sorrow
Upon the foot of motion.

BANQUO   *Realize its not safe to speak there.*   Look to the lady.
[LADY MACBETH *is carried out*
*talking about clothes, but rly about truth* And when we have our naked frailties hid, )the   125
That suffer in exposure, let us meet   *truth.*
And question this most bloody piece of work,
To know it further. Fears and scruples shake us.
In the great hand of God I stand, and thence
Against the undivulged pretence I fight   130
Of treasonous malice.

73

They all join Banquo in swearing an oath to the cause of right. Whilst the others are dressing, Malcolm and Donalbain decide to flee – to England and Ireland, respectively.

| 132 | **briefly** quickly |
| | **put ... readiness** get dressed, get ready for action |
| 134 | **consort** associate |
| 135 | **office** action |
| 136 | **easy** easily |
| 137 | **Our separated ... safer** We shall be safer in future if we split up |
| 138–40 | **Where we ... bloody** Here we cannot tell what people are really thinking; those who are most closely related to Duncan are in the greatest danger |
| 140–2 | **This murderous ... aim** This fatal arrow that has been shot is still in the air, so we should try and make sure it doesn't hit us |
| 141 | **lighted** landed |
| 143 | **dainty of leave-taking** particular about saying goodbye |
| 144 | **warrant in** justification for |
| 145 | **steals itself** 1) takes itself off 2) steels itself, preparing for the worst |

Ross and an old man begin discussing the strange events in nature of the previous night.

| 2 | **Within ... time** in this period of time |
| 3 | **sore** dreadful |
| 4 | **Hath ... knowings** has made previous experiences seem insignificant |
| | **father** A form of address used for a much older man. |
| 5 | **heavens** sky |
| | **act** deeds |
| | **bloody stage** i.e. earth, the scene of bloodshed |

MACDUFF          And so do I.

ALL                                    So all.

MACBETH    Let's briefly put on manly readiness,) Get dressed.
            And meet i' th' hall together.

ALL                                        Well contented.

*[Exeunt all but* MALCOLM *and* DONALBAIN

MALCOLM    What will you do? Let's not consort with them.
            To show an unfelt sorrow is an office          135
            Which the false man does easy. I'll to England.

DONALBAIN  To Ireland I. Our separated fortune
            Shall keep us both the safer. Where we are,
            (There's daggers in men's smiles;) the near in blood,
            The nearer bloody.        └ Don't Appearance anyone
                                           trust
MALCOLM                   (This murderous shaft that's shot  140
            Hath not yet lighted,) and our safest way   not done yet.
            Is to avoid the aim. Therefore to horse,
            And let us not be dainty of leave-taking,
            But shift away. There's warrant in that theft
            Which steals itself, when there's no mercy left.   145

                                            *[Exeunt*


## Scene ④

*Enter* ROSS, *and an old man*

OLD MAN    ( Threescore and ten) I can remember well,
                    70
            Within the volume of which time I have seen
            Hours dreadful, and things strange; but this sore
                night
            Hath trifled former knowings.

ROSS                              Ha, good father,
            Thou seest the heavens, as troubled with man's act,  5
            Threatens his bloody stage. By th' clock 'tis day,

Ross and the old man add to the description that Lennox has already given. Macduff confirms that the guards were responsible for Duncan's death, and says that Malcolm and Donalbain are suspected of arranging it.

| | |
|---|---|
| 7 | **travelling lamp** sun moving across the sky |
| 8 | **predominance** superior influence |
| 8–10 | **Is't ... kiss it?** Is it because night is more powerful, or because day is ashamed to look on the murder that it is dark now when it should be light? |
| 12 | **towering ... place** flying upwards to her highest point |
| 13 | **mousing owl** An owl usually flies low to catch mice. |
| | **hawked at** swooped down on as a hawk might do |
| 15 | **minions** choicest |
| | **Turned ... nature** became uncontrollable |
| 17 | **Contending 'gainst obedience** disregarding orders |
| 20 | **looked upon't** I saw it |
| 21 | **How ... now?** How are things? What news? |
| 24 | **What ... pretend?** What did they hope to get out of it? |
| | **suborned** bribed |
| 27 | **'Gainst nature still** Another example of the unnatural |
| 28–9 | **Thriftless ... means!** An unprofitable ambition to feed ravenously on the one who sustains you! |
| 29–30 | **Then ... Macbeth** Malcolm and Donalbain were Duncan's sons, so the line of succession should have gone through them, with Malcolm, the older brother, becoming king. But, because they ran away, they were suspected of murdering their father. So the succession went to Macbeth, who was Duncan's cousin, as can be seen from the family tree diagram on page x. |

And yet dark night strangles the travelling lamp.
Is't night's predominance, or the day's shame,
That darkness does the face of earth entomb,
When living light should kiss it?

OLD MAN                                         'Tis unnatural,          10
Even like the deed that's done. On Tuesday last,
A falcon towering in her pride of place                   *possitive to*
Was by a mousing owl hawked at, and killed.              *negative*
                                                          *animal*
ROSS      And Duncan's horses – a thing most strange and    *imagery.*
             certain –
Beauteous and swift, the minions of their race,          15
Turned wild in nature, broke their stalls, flung out,
Contending 'gainst obedience, as they would make
War with mankind.
                                                          *Horses*
OLD MAN                          'Tis said they ate each other.  *represent*
                                                          *his kin*
ROSS      They did so, to th' amazement of mine eyes       *civil war.*
That looked upon't. Here comes the good Macduff. 20

*Enter* MACDUFF

How goes the world sir, now?

MACDUFF                          Why, see you not?

ROSS      Is't known who did this more than bloody deed?

MACDUFF   Those that Macbeth hath slain.            *equivocating - doesnt*
                                                    *believe it, but can't talk*
ROSS                             Alas the day,      *openly about*
What good could they pretend?                       *it.*

MACDUFF                          They were suborned.
Malcolm and Donalbain, the King's two sons,              25
Are stolen away and fled, which puts upon them
Suspicion of the deed.)  *suspicion on them.*

ROSS      *thoughtless ambition*      'Gainst nature still.
Thriftless ambition) that will ravin up
Thine own life's means! Then 'tis most like
The sovereignty will fall upon Macbeth.                  30

Macduff tells them that Macbeth has been named to succeed Duncan, but he (Macduff) will not attend the coronation.

**31**    **named** elected

**Scone** (pronounced 'Skoon') i.e. where Scottish kings were crowned

**33**    **Colme-kill** The royal burial-ground on the island of Iona.

**36**    **Fife** (the site of Macduff's castle)

**thither** to Scone

**37**    **Well ... there** Macduff uses the word 'well' twice. He means exactly the opposite. This is an example of **irony** (see Glossary p. 241).

**38**    **Lest ... new!** For fear that the old reign will prove to have been more comfortable than the new!

**40**    **benison** blessing

MACDUFF   He is already named, and gone to Scone
          To be invested. ) *He will be made king Macbeth*

ROSS      Where is Duncan's body? *Macbeth*

MACDUFF                           Carried to Colme-kill,
          The sacred storehouse of his predecessors,
          And guardian of their bones.

ROSS                                Will you to Scone?   35

MACDUFF   No cousin, I'll to Fife.) *to his family*

ROSS                      Well, I will thither.

MACDUFF   Well, may you see things well done there. Adieu.
*Opposite to Macbeth* Lest our old robes sit easier than our new! ) *Regret*

ROSS      Farewell, father.

OLD MAN   God's benison go with you, and with those   40
          That would make good of bad, and friends of foes.

                                              [*Exeunt*

*He won't go see the new king,
nor he'll see his family
He's suspicious*

# Act 2 scenes 3 and 4

## Staging scene 3

*Macbeth* was written for performance in the Globe Theatre. You can see what this looked like on pages xiv–xvii. We can show the acting area as a plan like the one at the bottom of the page.

At the beginning of each scene the stage would have been empty. Actors could enter from three different places: the two doorways (marked 'entrance' on the plan), and the inner stage, through the curtains.

**Work in a group of four**

1   Discuss the whole scene. Decide what is outside each of the doors and what is in the inner stage.

2   Each take one of these sections of the scene:

   lines 1–42    lines 43–85    lines 85–117    lines 117–145

3   Read your lines carefully to get a picture in your mind of where the characters are and what they do as the story develops.

4   Choose a key moment in the scene and draw a plan to show where all the actors are at that particular moment. Only put in the characters who are important at that moment.

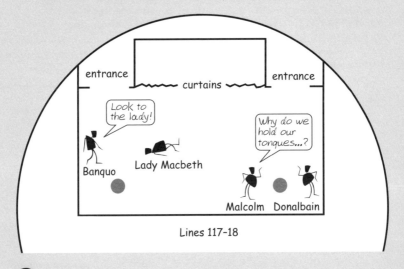

Lines 117–18

5 Underneath your diagram, write an explanation of how each character moves and reacts during those lines.

6 When you have all finished, share and discuss your ideas.

# Investigating the murder of Duncan

Shakespeare was not afraid of showing people being killed on stage. Indeed, later in the play, we see a number of deaths. But the murder of Duncan is only reported and we have to imagine what happens. If you want to get a clear picture of what happened, you have be a bit of a detective.

**Work with a partner**

1 The table below sets out the lines from scenes 2 and 3 that provide the information you need. Copy the table onto a large sheet of paper.

2 Go through the scenes and fill in the spaces in the right-hand column. The first one has been done for you as an example.

| Scene | Lines | Information they provide |
|-------|-------|--------------------------|
| 2 | 4–12 | Lady Macbeth drugged Duncan's personal servants, so that they were unconscious, and put their daggers out ready for Macbeth to use. |
| | 20–7 | |
| | 46–55 | |
| 3 | 64–70 | |
| | 98–116 | |

3 When you have finished, use the information you have collected to produce a report for the rest of the class.

## *Where were you at the time of the murder?*

Any of the characters who appear in scene 3 could have murdered Duncan:

**Characters:**   Porter       Macduff      Lennox       Macbeth
                  Lady Macbeth Banquo       Donalbain    Malcolm

Each of these people had the opportunity to commit the murder.

**Work with a partner**

1 You have been given the job of investigating the murder. Each choose a different character from the list.

2 You question your chosen character to find out where they were and what they were doing at the time of Duncan's death. Write about 50 words reporting what he or she says.

3 Share your reports.

4 Do the same for two of the other characters.

# Why did Malcolm and Donalbain run away?

By the end of Act 2 Duncan's two sons, Malcolm and Donalbain, have run away from Scotland. Why?

**Work on your own**

1 In scene 3, we see Malcolm and Donalbain 'thinking on their feet'. While everyone else is distracted by Lady Macbeth's fainting fit, they exchange a few words. Read scene 3 lines 118–23 again.

2 What do these lines tell us about:

   a why they are not speaking?

   b why they are not expressing their grief?

   c why they are worried about their own situation?

3 Now look at lines 134–45. The two have had a few moments to collect their thoughts.

   a What have they decided to do?

   b Why?

   c What does Malcolm mean when he says the following words?

   *This murderous shaft that's shot*
   *Hath not yet lighted, and our safest way*
   *Is to avoid the aim.*

4 In scene 4 we find out why other people think they ran away. What do lines 24–7 tell us about this?

# Plot summary quiz

The 12 short quotations below sum up the story of scenes 3 and 4.

1 Work out the correct order for them.
2 Work out who said each one.

**A**

Is the King stirring, worthy Thane?

**B**

Knock, knock, knock. Who's there, i' th' name of Beelzebub?

**C**

…let us meet
And question this most bloody piece of work…

**D**

…let us not be dainty of leave-taking,
But shift away.

**E**

Let's away; our tears
Are not yet brewed.

**F**

Malcolm and Donalbain, the King's two sons,
Are stolen away and fled…

**G**

O Banquo, Banquo,
Our royal master's murdered.

**H**

O horror, horror, horror!

**I**

O yet I do repent me of my fury,
That I did kill them.

**J**

Ring the alarum-bell.

**K**

The spring, the head, the fountain of your blood
Is stopped…

**L**

Those of his chamber, as it seemed, had done't.

Macbeth is king, and Banquo suspects him of foul play. Macbeth and Lady Macbeth make a great show of inviting Banquo to a formal banquet.

| | |
|---|---|
| **3** | **play'dst** plotted |
| **4** | **It** i.e. the succession |
| | **stand in thy posterity** remain in your family |
| **5** | **root** beginning, source |
| **6** | **them** the witches |
| **7** | **shine** show favour |
| **8** | **verities** truths |
| **9** | **oracles** prophets |
| **SD** | ***Sennet*** A trumpet call signalling the beginning of a procession. |
| **13** | **all-thing unbecoming** totally unfitting |
| **14** | **solemn** formal |
| **15** | **I'll** The invitation is personal. |
| **16** | **to the which** (your command) |
| **16–18** | **my duties ... knit** I am bound with an unbreakable tie to carry out |
| **21** | **We** (the royal plural) |
| | **else** otherwise |

# Act Three

## Scene 1

*Enter* BANQUO

BANQUO      Thou hast it now: King, Cawdor, Glamis, all
As the weird women promised, and I fear
Thou play'dst most foully for't; yet it was said
It should not stand in thy posterity,     *fertility*
But that myself should be the <u>root</u> and father    5
Of many kings. If there come truth from them –
As upon thee, Macbeth, their speeches shine –
Why by the verities on thee made good      *Briefly tempted*
May they not be my oracles as well,      *but*    10
And set me up in hope? <u>But hush, no more.</u>   *stops himself*

*moderation*
*& He's not Macbeth*

*Sennet sounded. Enter* MACBETH *as King,* LADY
MACBETH *as Queen,* LENNOX, ROSS, *lords, ladies and
attendants*

MACBETH      Here's our chief guest.

L. MACBETH               If he had been forgotten,
It had been as a gap in our great feast,    *Foreshadowing*
And all-thing unbecoming.      *wouldn't be the*
*same without B.*

MACBETH      Tonight we hold a solemn supper<u>, sir,</u>
( And I'll request your presence.) *distances himself*
           *nice*

BANQUO                  Let your <u>Highness</u>    15
Command upon me, to the which my <u>duties</u>
Are with a most indissoluble tie    *friendship*
For ever knit.

MACBETH      Ride you this afternoon? – *needs to know to kill him*

BANQUO      Ay, my good lord.      20

MACBETH      We should have else desired your good advice,

Banquo is going riding with Fleance before the banquet. Macbeth chats with them before they leave and makes sure that Fleance is going too. When they have left, Macbeth asks to be left alone so that he will appreciate company later. He admits that Banquo worries him.

| | |
|---|---|
| **22** | **Which ... prosperous** which has always been both wise and profitable |
| **23** | **take tomorrow** The text is unclear – either 'take (it) the advice' or 'talk' tomorrow. |
| **26** | **'Twixt ... supper** between now and suppertime |
| | **Go ... better** If my horse is not fast enough |
| **27** | **become ... night** ride on in darkness |
| **28** | **twain** two |
| | **Fail not** Do not miss |
| **30** | **our bloody cousins** Malcolm and Donalbain |
| | **bestowed** lodged |
| **32** | **parricide** patricide, murder of their father |
| **33** | **strange invention** stories of Macbeth's guilt |
| **34–5** | **cause ... jointly** matters of state demanding our joint attention |
| **35** | **Hie** Hurry |
| **37** | **our time ... upon's** it is time we went |
| **42–3** | **To make ... welcome** So that you will enjoy our company all the more |
| **44** | **While then** Until then |
| **45** | **Sirrah** A term used when addressing someone socially inferior. |
| **45–6** | **Attend ... pleasure?** Are those men waiting to speak with us? |
| **47** | **without** outside |
| **48–9** | **To be thus ... thus** To be king in this way is worth nothing unless I am safely king |
| **50** | **Stick deep** torment us |
| **50–1** | **in his ... feared** he has a king-like quality which might cause problems |

Which still hath been both grave and prosperous,
In this day's council. But we'll take tomorrow.
Is't far you ride?

BANQUO          As far, my lord, as will fill up the time          25
'Twixt this and supper. Go not my horse the better,
*caught in* I must become a borrower of the night
*the night* For a dark hour or twain.

MACBETH                              ✳ Fail not our feast. *Don't miss*
                                                            *it!*

BANQUO          My lord, I will not.

MACBETH          We hear our bloody cousins are bestowed          30
In England and in Ireland, not confessing
Their cruel parricide, filling their hearers
With strange invention. But of that tomorrow,
When therewithal we shall have cause of state
*Shows B.* Craving us jointly. Hie you to horse. Adieu,          35
*and his* Till you return at night. (Goes Fleance with you? )*Finds out*
*son are close*                                                 *information.*
BANQUO          Ay my good lord; our time does call upon's.

MACBETH          I wish your horses swift, and sure of foot;
And so I do commend you to their backs.
Farewell.                                   [*Exit* BANQUO    40

Let every man be master of his time
Till seven at night. To make society
The sweeter welcome, we will keep ourself
Till supper-time alone. While then, God be with
    you!

                [*Exeunt all but* MACBETH *and* SERVANT

*inferior* Sirrah, a word with you. Attend those men          45
    Our pleasure?

SERVANT          They are, my lord, without the palace gate.

MACBETH          Bring them before us.            [*Exit* SERVANT

*doesn't* To be thus is nothing,
*feel safe* But to be safely thus. Our fears in Banquo
Stick deep, and in his royalty of nature          *Kings*     50
Reigns that which would be feared. 'Tis much he
    dares,

✳ We don't know his plans because he doesnt
    tell L. Macbeth                                            87

Macbeth is bitter that, if the witches' prophecies come true, he has killed Duncan for the benefit of Banquo's descendants. He speaks with two murderers, assuring them that their bad luck is somehow Banquo's fault.

**52**      **to that ... temper** in addition to the fearless quality

**53**      **He hath ... valour** he has common sense which persuades his bravery

**56**      **My Genius is rebuked** my guardian spirit is checked

**57**      **chid** reproached

**61–2**    **fruitless ... sceptre** Macbeth and Banquo have been told that Macbeth will inherit the crown, but after him, Banquo's children will inherit.

**62**      **gripe** grip

**63**      **with ... hand** by someone not of my line, not a descendant of mine

**65**      **For Banquo's ... mind** I have defiled my mind for the benefit of Banquo's heirs

**67–70**   **Put rancours ... kings** ruined my peace of mind just for them and I have given my immortal soul to the devil to allow them to be kings

**67**      **rancours** bitterness

**68**      **eternal jewel** immortal soul

**69**      **common enemy of man** i.e. the devil

**70**      **seed** children

**71**      **come Fate ... list** let Fate enter the tournament, the scene of contest (an example of **personification**, see Glossary p. 241)

**72**      **champion ... utterance** This is not clear. It either means 'challenge me in a fight to the death' or 'support me in a fight to the death'.

**78**      **under fortune** below what you deserve

**79**      **made good** showed

**80**      **passed in probation** proved to you

**81**      **How ... hand** how you had been tricked

         **instruments** means

And to that dauntless temper of his mind
He hath a wisdom that doth guide his valour
To act in safety. There is none but he
Whose being I do fear, and under him                    55
My Genius is rebuked as, it is said,
Mark Antony's was by Caesar. He chid the sisters
When first they put the name of king upon me,
And bade them speak to him. Then, prophet-like,
They hailed him <u>father</u> to a <u>line of kings</u>.         60
Upon my head they placed a <u>fruitless crown</u>,
And put a <u>barren</u> sceptre in my gripe,
Thence to be wrenched with an unlineal hand,
No son of mine succeeding. If't be so,
For <u>Banquo</u>'s issue have I filed my mind,             65
For them the gracious <u>Duncan</u> have I murdered,
Put rancours in the vessel of my peace
Only for them, and mine (eternal jewel)
Given to the common (enemy of man,)
To make them kings, the <u>seed</u> of Banquo kings.       70
Rather than so, come Fate into the list
And champion me to th' utterance. Who's there?

*Enter servant, and two* MURDERERS

Now go to the door, and stay there till we call.

                                          *[Exit servant*

Was it not yesterday we spoke together?

**1ST M.**    It was, so please your Highness.

**MACBETH**                           Well then, now     75
Have you considered of my speeches? Know
That it was he in the times past which held you
So under fortune, which you thought had been
Our innocent self. This I made good to you
In our last conference, (passed in probation) with you,                                                   80
How you were borne in hand, how crossed; the instruments,

Macbeth urges the murderers to take revenge on Banquo and his family. He tries to persuade them that becoming assassins will prove that they are 'real' men.

**82**    **wrought with** used

**83**    **To half ... crazed** even to a half-wit and a fool

**88**    **so gospelled** so religious, such readers of the gospels

**89**    **this good man** Here, 'good' is an example of **irony** (see Glossary p. 241).

         **his issue** his children

**91**    **beggared yours** made your children beggars

**94**    **shoughs** shaggy dogs

         **water-rugs** rough-haired water-dogs

         **demi-wolves** cross-breeds or dogs that look more like wolves

**94–5**  **clept ... dogs** all referred to as 'dogs'

**95**    **valued file** list that indicates the individual qualities of each breed

**96**    **subtle** clever

**97**    **housekeeper** watch-dog

**98–9**  **According ... closed** depending on the particular quality which generous nature has given to him

**100–1** **Particular ... alike** a special name added to the general catalogue which just listed 'dog'

**102–3** **if you ... say't** if you aren't the lowest of the low, then tell me

**104–5** **I will ... off** I will give you a job to do that will get rid of your enemy

**105**   **execution** 1) killing 2) carrying out the business – a **play on words** (see Glossary p. 242)

         **takes ... off** 1) takes away 2) kills

**107**   **Who ... his life** our health seems fragile as long as he is alive

**109–11** **Whom ... the world** I have been so angered by all the many knocks and blows of this life that I can take no more and I don't care what I do to get revenge

**112**   **tugged** pulled about

Who wrought with them, and all things else that
    might
To half a soul, and to a notion crazed,
Say 'Thus did Banquo.'

1ST M.                 You made it known to us.

MACBETH  I did so, and went further, which is now    85
*learned from* Our point of second meeting. Do you find
*L. Macbeth* Your patience so predominant in your nature,
*Goes thru* That you can let this go? Are you so gospelled
*same process* To pray for this good man, and for his issue,
*to convince* Whose heavy hand hath bowed you to the grave,  90
*the murderers* And beggared yours for ever?

1ST M.                     We are men, my liege.

MACBETH  Ay, in the catalogue ye go for men,
*nothing* As hounds, and greyhounds, mongrels, spaniels, curs,
*satisfies him* Shoughs, water-rugs, and demi-wolves are clept
All by the name of dogs. The valued file    95
Distinguishes the swift, the slow, the subtle,
The housekeeper, the hunter, every one
According to the gift which bounteous nature
Hath in him closed, whereby he does receive
Particular addition, from the bill    100
That writes them all alike. And so of men.
Now, if you have a station in the file,
*convinces the* Not i' th' worst rank of manhood, say't,
*murderers that* And I will put that business in your bosoms,
*. is their* Whose execution takes your enemy off,   105
*enemy* Grapples you to the heart and love of us,
Who wear our health but sickly in his life,
(Which in his death were perfect.) *perfect if he was dead.*

2ND M.                 I am one, my liege,
*hates the* Whom the vile blows and buffets of the world
*world* Have so incensed, that I am reckless what  110
I do to spite the world.

1ST M.               And I another
So weary with disasters, tugged with fortune,

Macbeth explains that he has the power to kill Banquo openly but that this would produce problems for him. This is why he is appealing to them. The murderers agree to kill Banquo and Fleance.

**114**  **To mend ... on't** to improve it or do away with it altogether

**116**  **bloody distance** space between swordsmen

**116–18**  **in such ... life** he is so close that every minute he lives is threatening my life

**118–23**  **though ... struck down** although I could quite simply get rid of him openly and justify it, I must not do it because there are certain friends common to both of us, whose affection I cannot afford to lose, but I would have to mourn the death of the man I had killed

**119**  **bare-faced** open, undisguised

**120**  **bid my ... it** simply say it is what I want

**avouch** justify

**122**  **but wail** but must bewail, mourn

**124**  **I ... love** call upon your help

**125**  **Masking ... eye** hiding the deal from the public

**126**  **sundry weighty** various important

**130**  **Acquaint ... time** make known to you precisely the ideal time

**131**  **on't** of the murder

**132**  **something** some distance away

**always thought** always bearing in mind

**133**  **I require a clearness** I must be clear of suspicion

**134**  **no rubs nor botches** no roughness and no bungling

**136**  **absence** death

**material** important

**137**  **embrace** share

**138**  **Resolve yourselves apart** Go away and prepare yourselves

**140**  **I'll call ... straight** I'll join you straight away

**Abide within** Wait in an inner room

That I would set my life on any chance
To mend it or be rid on't.

MACBETH                                    Both of you
Know Banquo was your enemy.

MURDERERS                        *Fight imagery*   True, my lord.   115

MACBETH   (So is he mine; and in such bloody distance
That every minute of his being thrusts   *Truth,*
Against my near'st of life;) and though I could
*Appearance/*   With bare-faced power sweep him from my sight,
*reality.*   And bid my will avouch it, yet I must not,   120
*pretends to*   For certain friends that are both his and mine,
*be nice*   Whose loves I may not drop, but wail his fall
*but kills his*   Who I myself struck down. And thence it is
*Friend.*   That I to your assistance do make love,
(Masking the business from the common eye)   125
For sundry weighty reasons.

2ND M.                                  We shall, my lord,
Perform what you command us.

1ST M.                                          Though our lives –

MACBETH   Your spirits shine through you. Within this hour
    at most,
*Banquo's*   I will advise you where to plant yourselves,
*son would*   Acquaint you with the perfect spy o' th' time,   130
*become*   (The moment on't, for't must be done tonight,)
*King*   And something from the palace; always thought
That I require a clearness; and with him –
To leave no rubs nor botches in the work –
Fleance his son, that keeps him company,   135
Whose absence is no less material to me
Than is his father's, must embrace the fate
Of that dark hour. Resolve yourselves apart,
I'll come to you anon.

MURDERERS                        We are resolved, my lord.

MACBETH   I'll call upon you straight. Abide within.   140

                              [*Exeunt* MURDERERS

*Is Macbeth the 3rd M.?*

93

Lady Macbeth is as uneasy about their position as Macbeth is, but she presents a different face to her husband.

**5–6**   **Nought's ... content** Nothing has been gained, all has been lost, when we have got what we wanted but do not have peace of mind

**7**   **that ... destroy** i.e. our victim, Duncan

**8**   **doubtful** fearful

**10**   **sorriest fancies** saddest images

**11–12**   **Using ... think on** becoming preoccupied with the very thoughts which should have died with the subject of them

**12–13**   **Things ... regard** What cannot be changed should be ignored

**14**   **scorched** slashed, wounded

**15**   **close** heal up

**15–16**   **whilst our ... tooth** while our feeble wickedness means that we are as threatened as we were before

**17**   **let ... disjoint** if we let everything fall apart

 **both the worlds** heaven and earth

**18**   **Ere** before

**19**   **affliction** suffering

**20**   **That ... nightly** that disrupt our sleep with terror every night

 **Better ... dead** It would be better to be lying with the dead (Duncan)

It is concluded. Banquo, thy soul's <u>flight</u>,
If it find heaven, must find it out to<u>night.</u>

*Banquo goes to heaven*

[*Exit*

## Scene 2

*Enter* LADY MACBETH *and a* SERVANT

L. MACBETH  Is Banquo gone from court?

SERVANT  Ay, madam, but returns again tonight.

L. MACBETH  Say to the King, I would attend his leisure
For a few words.  *not close anymore*

SERVANT  Madam, I will.

[*Exit*

L. MACBETH                      Nought's had, all's spent,  *p.*  5
*worried* Where our desire is got without content.  *87 - line 48*
*not happy* 'Tis safer to be that which we destroy,
Than by destruction dwell in doubtful j<u>oy.</u>  *important thought*

*Enter* MACBETH

*changes into having control* How now my lord? Why do you keep alone,
Of sorriest fancies your companions making,  10
Using those thoughts which should indeed have
     died
With them they think on? Things without all
     remedy
Should be without regard. What's done is done.  *quote.*

MACBETH  We have scorched the snake, *Duncan* not killed it.

*everybody in their way is evil* She'll close, and be herself, whilst our poor malice  15
Remains in danger of her former tooth.
But let the frame of things disjoint, both the
     worlds suffer,
Ere we will eat our meal in fear, and sleep
*not sleeping well.* In the affliction of these terrible dreams
That shake us nightly. Better be with the dead,  20

*envy Duncan.*            *they agree.*

95

Lady Macbeth urges her husband to put the past behind him. Macbeth hints that he has a plan in hand that will be carried out that evening. He will not give Lady Macbeth the details but he says that she will approve.

| | |
|---|---|
| **21** | **Whom ... to peace** whom we sent to the peace which is death, thinking to achieve our peace of mind, our position |
| **22–3** | **Than ... ecstasy** than to lie tormented, tossing and turning |
| **26** | **Malice domestic** civil war |
| | **foreign levy** an army to make war |
| **28** | **sleek ... looks** smooth over your irritable appearance |
| **31** | **Let your ... Banquo** Make sure to remember Banquo particularly |
| **32** | **Present him eminence** honour him as chief guest |
| | **Unsafe ... streams** we are unsafe at the moment and so we must bathe our titles in streams of flattery to others |
| **33** | **lave** wash |
| **34–5** | **and make ... hearts** and turn our faces into masks for our hearts |
| **39** | **nature's ... eterne** 1) there won't always be suitable descendants 2) they are not immortal |
| **40** | **are assailable** can be dealt with |
| **41** | **jocund** cheerful |
| **41–2** | **Ere ... flight** Before the bat has darted through the cloisters |
| | **ere ... summons** before, ordered by evil Hecate, Queen of the Witches |
| **43** | **shard-borne beetle** beetle flying on his scaly wings |
| **43–4** | **with ... peal** with its sleepy humming sounds the curfew |
| **46** | **chuck** chick (used as term of affection) |
| **47** | **seeling night** concealing night (When a hawk was being trained its eyes were 'seeled', stitched shut, so that it was temporarily blind.) |
| **48** | **Scarf up** blindfold |
| **50** | **that great bond** the lease of life, the destiny embodied in the life of Banquo and Fleance |

Whom we, to gain our peace, have sent to peace,
Than on the torture of the mind to lie
In restless ecstasy. Duncan is in his grave,
After life's fitful fever he sleeps well.
Treason has done his worst: nor steel, nor poison,    25
Malice domestic, foreign levy, nothing,
Can touch him further.    *Svenu*

*Lots of treason everywhere*

*He wishes to be dead.*

L. MACBETH                    Come on –
Gentle my lord, sleek o'er your rugged looks,
Be bright and jovial among your guests tonight.

*Appearance of reality*

MACBETH    So shall I, love; and so I pray be you.    30
Let your remembrance apply to Banquo,
Present him eminence both with eye and tongue –
Unsafe the while that we must lave our honours
In these flattering streams, and make our faces
Vizards to our hearts, disguising what they are.    35

*pretend you like B.*

L. MACBETH    You must leave this.    *Conceal don't feel*

MACBETH    O full of scorpions is my mind, dear wife.
Thou know'st that Banquo, and his Fleance, lives.

*evil, poisonous caused by ambition*

L. MACBETH    But in them nature's copy's not eterne.    *won't live forever*

MACBETH    There's comfort yet, they are assailable;    40
Then be thou jocund. Ere the bat hath flown
His cloistered flight; ere to black Hecate's
    summons
The shard-borne beetle with his drowsy hums
Hath rung night's yawning peal, there shall be
    done
A deed of dreadful note.

*something bad will happen*

L. MACBETH                    What's to be done?    45

MACBETH    Be innocent of the knowledge, dearest chuck,
Till thou applaud the deed. Come, seeling night,
Scarf up the tender eye of pitiful day,
And with thy bloody and invisible hand
Cancel and tear to pieces that great bond    50

*Keeps it from her*

- Uses the night to conceal things

Macbeth's mood often changes. He has managed to persuade himself that dealing with Banquo and Fleance will solve his problems.

51 **pale** fearful

**Light thickens** Light is changing to twilight, it is growing dark

52 **Makes wing** is flying

54 **Whiles ... rouse** and all the while, night's evil prepares for its victims

# Act 3 scenes 1 and 2

In these two scenes, we begin to see the workings of Macbeth's mind as he plots the murder of Banquo and Fleance.

In scene 1 we find out:

- why he thinks he must kill Banquo and Fleance
- the reasons he has given the two killers
- how he wants them to do their work.

In scene 2 we learn how he feels about what he is planning.

We can begin to plot what we learn in these two scenes in a diagram like the one below.

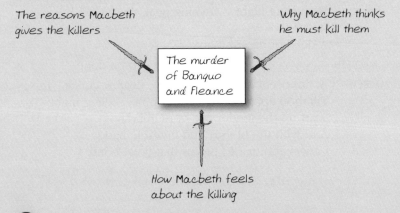

The reasons Macbeth gives the killers

Why Macbeth thinks he must kill them

The murder of Banquo and Fleance

How Macbeth feels about the killing

Which keeps me pale. Light thickens, and the crow
Makes wing to th' rooky wood.
Good things of day begin to droop and drowse,
Whiles night's black agents to their preys do rouse.
Thou marvell'st at my words; but hold thee still.    55
(Things bad begun make strong themselves by ill)
So prithee go with me.)

*solve bad things with more bad things* [handwritten annotation]

- Talks about evil things [handwritten annotation]

[*Exeunt*

## Scene 1

### Work with a partner

1   Take a large sheet of paper and copy out the diagram at the bottom of page 98. Put it in the centre of your paper and leave plenty of room for adding things.

2   Read again Macbeth's speech on pages 87 and 89 (lines 48–72). This tells us his thoughts about why he must have Banquo and Fleance killed. Add to your diagram all the reasons you can find, like this:

The witches' prophecy

Why Macbeth thinks he must kill them

99

**3** For each reason, find a quotation that backs it up:

They hailed him father to a line of kings ... No son of mine succeeding.

The witches' prophecy

**4** Now read Macbeth's conversation with the murderers (pages 89–93 lines 74–139).

**5** Add to your diagram the reasons that Macbeth has given the murderers for killing Banquo.

**6** For each reason give a short quotation, as before.

## Scene 2

In this scene Macbeth talks to his wife about his feelings, but he doesn't tell her straight out what he is planning:

*Be innocent of the knowledge, dearest chuck,*
*Till thou applaud the deed.*
(lines 46–7)

To express himself he uses a number of striking images. Some of these are set out in the table opposite.

**Work with the same partner as before**

1   Copy the table onto a large sheet of paper, leaving plenty of space for your answers.

2   Read the whole scene carefully and then fill in the spaces in the middle column with the missing quotations.

3   Now complete the right-hand column by adding your explanation of what the image means to you.

| Lines | Quotation | Exploration |
|-------|-----------|-------------|
| 14–17 | We have scorched the snake, not killed it... | Macbeth thinks the dangers they still face, as they pursue their ambition, are like a snake. They have only cut its skin, but they haven't killed it yet, so they are still in danger. |
| 23–4 | Duncan is in his grave, After life's fitful fever he sleeps well... | |
| 34–5 | | |
| 37 | | |
| 47–8 | | |
| 53–4 | | |

# Completing your web diagram

Now use the ideas you have developed in the table to help you complete the third part of your web diagram: 'How Macbeth feels about the killing'.

The murderers lie in ambush while they wait for Banquo and Fleance to return to the palace.

**2–4**    **He needs ... just** We can trust him because he has told us our duties exactly as Macbeth directed

**6**    **lated** delayed

       **apace** quickly

**7**    **To gain ... inn** to reach the inn in good time

**7–8**    **near ... watch** the ones we have been waiting for are coming

**10**    **That ... expectation** who are expected at the banquet

**11**    **go about** are being taken round to the stables

**15**    **Stand to 't** Get ready to do it

**16**    **Let ... down** This is a **play on words** (see Glossary p. 242). 'It' refers to the rain, and also to their attack, i.e. a 'rain' of blows.

## Scene ❸

*Enter three* MURDERERS

1ST M.    But who did bid thee join with us?

*[handwritten: sends someone else because he doesn't want to do it.]*

3RD M.                                    Macbeth.

2ND M.    He needs not our mistrust, since he delivers
          Our offices, and what we have to do,          *[handwritten: He distrusts people.]*
          To the direction just.

1ST M.                        Then stand with us.
          The west yet glimmers with some streaks of day.          5
          Now spurs the lated traveller apace
          To gain the timely inn, and near approaches
          The subject of our watch.

3RD M.                        Hark! I hear horses.

BANQUO    [*Within*] Give us a light there, ho!    *[handwritten: It's dark]*

2ND M.                        Then 'tis he. The rest
          That are within the note of expectation          10
          Already are i' th' Court.

1ST M.                        His horses go about.

3RD M.    Almost a mile; but he does usually,
          So all men do, from hence to th' palace gate
          Make it their walk.

*Enter* BANQUO, *and* FLEANCE *with a torch*

2ND M.    A light, a light!

3RD M.            'Tis he.

1ST M.                    Stand to 't.          15

BANQUO    It will be rain tonight.          *[handwritten: Cool joke]*

1ST M.                        Let it come down.

                        [*They attack* BANQUO

Banquo is murdered. He just manages to tell Fleance to get away. In the confusion, Fleance escapes.

**20–1**   **We have ... affair** We have failed to carry out a good part of our task

Macbeth and Lady Macbeth welcome guests to the banquet. The First Murderer reports to Macbeth that Banquo has been killed.

**1**      **degrees** ranks, titles (which will determine their places at the table)

**1–2**    **At ... last** From beginning to end

**3**      **society** the guests

**4**      **keeps her state** remains in her chair of state, throne

**5**      **we ... welcome** we will ask her to welcome you

**6**      **Pronounce it** Announce the welcome

**7**      **my heart speaks** from my heart

**8**      **encounter thee** respond to you

**10**     **Be ... mirth** Enjoy yourselves freely

**13**     **'Tis ... within** It is better on the outside of you than inside him

*He knows Macbeth is behind this*

**BANQUO** O treachery! Fly good Fleance, fly, fly, fly!
Thou mayst revenge. O slave! *Loves his son*

[*Dies.* FLEANCE *escapes*

*protected by B*

**3RD M.** Who did strike out the light?

**1ST M.** Was't not the way?

**3RD M.** There's but one down; the son is fled.

**2ND M.** We have lost 20
Best half of our affair. ) *Half failed.*

**1ST M.** Well let's away, and say how much is done.

[*Exeunt*

## Scene 4

*A banquet prepared*

*Enter* MACBETH, LADY MACBETH, ROSS, LENNOX, *lords,
and attendants*

*Sit according to power.*

**MACBETH** You know your own degrees, sit down. At first
And last the hearty welcome. *First public appearance as King*

**LORDS** Thanks to your Majesty.

**MACBETH** Ourself will mingle with society,
And play the humble host. Our hostess keeps her
state, *mimic Duncan-* ~~hospitable~~
But in best time we will require her welcome. 5

**L. MACBETH** Pronounce it for me, sir, to all our friends, *Everybody's happy*
For my heart speaks, they are welcome.

*Enter* FIRST MURDERER *to the door* *will cause more shock later.*

**MACBETH** See, they encounter thee with their hearts' thanks.
Both sides are even. (Here I'll sit i' th' midst.) *Humble*
Be large in mirth. Anon we'll drink a measure 10
The table round. [*To* FIRST MURDERER ( There's blood
upon thy face. ) *Guilt → suffers consequences*

**1ST M.** 'Tis Banquo's then.

**MACBETH** 'Tis better thee without than he within.

105

Macbeth is displeased at the news of Fleance's escape. The murderer leaves and Macbeth turns his attention back to the banquet.

**18**      **the nonpareil** the best possible, the one without equal

**20**      **fit** mood, fit of terror

        **I had ... perfect** otherwise all would have been well

**22**      **the casing air** the air which surrounds us

**23**      **cabined, cribbed, confined** imprisoned in the smallest possible space

**23–4**      **bound in ... fears** contained by insolent doubts and fears

**25**      **bides** rests, stays

**26**      **trenched gashes** deep-cut slashes

**27**      **The least ... nature** any one of which would have killed him

**28**      **worm** young serpent

**29**      **Hath ... breed** in the future he will be a threat

**31**      **hear ourselves again** talk further

**32**      **the cheer** encouragement which a host should give

**32–4**      **The feast ... welcome** A feast is no better than a meal which is paid for unless the host keeps repeating, during the festivities, that his guests are welcome

**34**      **To feed ... home** If people only want to eat they can stay at home

**35–6**      **From ... without it** When away from home, the sociability of the host adds, like sauce, to the meal; a gathering of people would be sadly lacking without it

**36**      **Meeting** This word reflects 'meat' in the previous line to make a **play on words** (see Glossary p. 242).

        **Sweet remembrancer!** You give me a good reminder!

**37–8**      **Now ... appetite** Forget about indigestion – eat your fill

**38**      **health on both** a toast!

**39**      **Here ... roofed** We would have here the chief nobles of Scotland under one roof

**40**      **Were ... present** if gracious Banquo were here

Is he dispatched?

1ST M.    My lord, his throat is cut; that I did for him.   15

MACBETH    Thou art the best o' th' cut-throats, yet he's good

*Cut his throat for blood*

That did the like for Fleance. If thou didst it,

Thou art the nonpareil.

1ST M.             Most royal Sir,

Fleance is 'scaped.  *Terror*

MACBETH    Then comes my fit again; I had else been perfect,  20

Whole as the marble, founded as the rock,  *stable*

*pure*    As broad and general as the casing air; *Free*

But now I am cabined, cribbed, confined, bound in *imprissoned*

To saucy doubts and fears. But Banquo's safe? *irony*

1ST M.    Ay, my good lord, safe in a ditch he bides,  25

With twenty trenched gashes on his head,

The least a death to nature.  *Rekt*

*For Macbeth to feel guilt - to see what he imagines.*

MACBETH            Thanks for that.

There the grown serpent lies. The worm that's fled

Hath nature that in time will venom breed,

No teeth for th' present. Get thee gone. Tomorrow  30

We'll hear ourselves again.

                    [*Exit* MURDERER

L. MACBETH          My royal lord,

You do not give the cheer. The feast is sold

*Bad host being told off by the wife*

That is not often vouched, while 'tis a-making,

'Tis given with welcome. To feed were best at home.

From thence the sauce to meat is ceremony,  35

Meeting were bare without it.

*Audience sees the ghost - in Macbeth's perspective D.I*

[*Banquo's ghost enters, and sits in* MACBETH'*s seat*]

*nice to L. Macbeth*

MACBETH               Sweet remembrancer!

Now, good digestion wait on appetite,

And health on both.

LENNOX          May't please your Highness sit.

MACBETH    Here had we now our country's honour roofed,

Were the graced person of our Banquo present,  40

*MB's appearance with his subjects vs. reality - Banquo's dead*

Macbeth intends to sit down but sees Banquo's ghost in his seat. Macbeth's reaction to the ghost startles the guests, and Lady Macbeth makes excuses for her husband. She draws him aside and is scornful of his behaviour.

**41–2**   **Who may ... mischance** I prefer to criticise him for bad manners rather than sympathise with him for bad luck

**45**   **The table's full** All the seats are taken

**47**   **Here ... Highness?** Lennox points to the empty seat. He sees from Macbeth's reaction that something is wrong.

**48**   **Which ... this?** 1) Which of you is playing this trick on me? 2) Which of you killed Banquo?

**50**   **gory locks** bloody hair

**54**   **The fit is momentary** This condition is short-lived

      **Upon a thought** In a moment

**55**   **If much ... him** If you pay him a lot of attention

**56**   **offend** annoy

      **extend his passion** prolong his agitation

**59**   **O proper stuff!** What nonsense!

**60**   **painting ... fear** illusion of the sight you fear

**61**   **air-drawn dagger** 1) pictured in the air 2) drawn through the air

**62**   **flaws** outbursts of feeling

**63**   **Impostors** not comparable

**64**   **A woman's story** an old wives' tale

**65**   **Authorised ... grandam** where the story-teller says her grandmother can vouch for the truth of it

      **Shame itself** You are shame in person

|  | Who may I rather challenge for unkindness, |
|---|---|
|  | Than pity for mischance. |
| ROSS | His absence, sir, |

*ghost → supernatural*

|  | Lays blame upon his promise. Please 't your Highness |
|---|---|
|  | To grace us with your royal company. |
| MACBETH | The table's full. |
| LENNOX | Here is a place reserved, sir. 45 |
| MACBETH | Where? |
| LENNOX | Here my good lord. What is't that moves your Highness? |
| MACBETH | Which of you have done this? |

*Irony — who put this ded body here — who killed B.?*

| LORDS | What, my good lord? |
|---|---|
| MACBETH | [*To Banquo's ghost*] Thou canst not say I did it; never shake |
|  | Thy gory locks at me. 50 |

*Blood - guilt.*

| ROSS | Gentlemen rise, his Highness is not well. |
|---|---|
| L. MACBETH | Sit, worthy friends. My lord is often thus, |

*L. Macbeth (protects him / takes control)*

|  | And hath been from his youth. Pray you keep seat. |
|---|---|
|  | The fit is momentary. Upon a thought |
|  | He will again be well. If much you note him, |
|  | You shall offend him, and extend his passion. |
|  | Feed, and regard him not. – Are you a man? |

*Similar to when she fainted to protece Macbeth, uses the same technique as before.*

| MACBETH | Ay, and a bold one, that dare look on that |
|---|---|
|  | Which might appal the devil. |
| L. MACBETH | O proper stuff! |

*not real*

|  | This is the very painting of your fear. |
|---|---|
|  | This is the air-drawn dagger which you said |
|  | Led you to Duncan. O these flaws and starts, |
|  | Impostors to true fear, would well become |
|  | A woman's story at a winter's fire, |
|  | Authorised by her grandam. Shame itself, 65 |
|  | Why do you make such faces? When all's done, |
|  | You look but on a stool. |

*Doesn't work indicates Macbeth has changed.*

*Doesn't see the gost bc. She's not guilty*

| MACBETH | Prithee see there. Behold, look, lo – how say you? |
|---|---|

*. Open to the interpretation of the reader. Doesnt say ghosts exist or not.*

109

When the ghost leaves, Macbeth rejoins his guests, but it reappears and Macbeth's 'fit' returns.

| | |
|---|---|
| **70** | **charnel-houses** tombs, burial places |
| **71–2** | **our ... kites** our only memorials will be the stomachs of kites |
| **72** | **maws** stomachs |
| | **kites** birds which feed mainly on carrion, dead flesh. |
| | **unmanned** turned feeble, without the qualities of manliness |
| | **folly** madness |
| **75** | **Ere ... weal** before humane law cleansed society |
| | **weal** welfare, general good |
| **77–8** | **The time ... That** Formerly, in earlier times |
| **80** | **mortal ... crowns** fatal wounds on their heads |
| **84** | **muse** wonder at |
| **90** | **thirst** 1) must drink 2) long for |
| **91** | **all to all** good wishes to everyone |
| | **duties ... pledge** loyalty and the toast |
| **94** | **speculation** power of sight |

*he'll never sleep .*

Why what care I? If thou canst nod, speak too.
If charnel-houses and our graves must send          70
Those that we bury back, our monuments
Shall be the maws of kites.

                                     *[Exit Ghost*

L. MACBETH                     What, quite unmanned in folly?

MACBETH    If I stand here, I saw him.

L. MACBETH                      Fie for shame!

MACBETH    Blood hath been shed ere now, i' th' olden time,

*breakdown*

              Ere human statute purged the gentle weal;          75

*§ murdered people come back to life .*

              Ay, and since too, murders have been performed
Too terrible for the ear. The time has been
That, when the brains were out, the man would die,

*vividly pictures Banquo*

And there an end. But now they rise again
With twenty mortal murders on their crowns,          80
And push us from our stools. This is more strange
Than such a murder is.   *nobody knows Banquo is dead, people stop trusting him*

L. MACBETH                  My worthy lord,
Your noble friends do lack you.   *→ Hosting a party*

MACBETH                    I do forget.

Do not muse at me, my most worthy friends,

*He's fine*

(I have a strange infirmity, which is nothing )          85
To those that know me. Come, love and health to all,
Then I'll sit down. Give me some wine fill full.

*Enter Ghost*

I drink to the general joy o' the whole table,   *Linked murder §*
And to our dear friend Banquo,(whom we miss.  *Banquo .*
Would he were here.) To all, and him, we thirst,          90
And all to all.

LORDS                Our duties, and the pledge.

MACBETH    Avaunt, and quit my sight, let the earth hide thee!
Thy bones are marrowless, thy blood is cold;
Thou hast no speculation in those eyes
Which thou dost glare with!   *mad*

Lady Macbeth again makes excuses for Macbeth's behaviour. The ghost leaves again and Macbeth is prepared to continue with the banquet, but Lady Macbeth urges the guests to leave. She fears Macbeth will say too much.

| | |
|---|---|
| **96** | **But as ... custom** just as something that happens from time to time |
| **98** | **What ... I dare** Whatever any man may dare, I dare it too |
| **99** | **like** in the form of |
| **100** | **armed** (with a horn and in armour) |
| | **Hyrcan tiger** Hyrcania was a region of eastern Europe believed to be full of wild beasts. |
| **101** | **Take any ... that** appear in any other form but that of Banquo |
| **103** | **dare ... sword** challenge me in a fight to the death |
| **104** | **If trembling ... then** if you find fear in me then |
| | **protest me** proclaim I am |
| **105** | **The baby ... girl** a baby girl |
| **106** | **Unreal mockery, hence!** pretence which mocks me, go! |
| **109** | **most admired disorder** the most amazing lack of self-control |
| **110** | **overcome us** pass over us, threaten |
| **111–12** | **strange ... owe** realise I do not know my own nature |
| **112** | **owe** possess |
| **114** | **the natural ... cheeks** your natural colour |
| **115** | **mine ... fear** mine has turned pale |
| | **blanched** whitened |
| **117** | **At once, good night** Good night to all of you |
| **118** | **Stand ... going** Do not wait to leave in the correct order of rank |
| **121** | **It will have blood** (Banquo's murder) |
| **122** | **Stones ... speak** These disturbances in nature show that all is not well and tend to mean that worse is to come |

L. MACBETH                              Think of this, good peers,    95
*normal.* But as a thing of custom. 'Tis no other,
Only it spoils the pleasure of the time.

MACBETH   What man dare, I dare. *Said when he killed Duncan.*
*Talks to* Approach thou like the rugged Russian bear,
*Banquo.* The armed rhinoceros, or th' Hyrcan tiger;    100
Take any shape but that, and my firm nerves
Shall never tremble. Or be alive again,
And dare me to the desert with thy sword:
If trembling I inhabit then, protest me
The baby of a girl. Hence, horrible shadow,    105
Unreal mockery, hence!

[*Exit Ghost*

Why, so; being gone,
I am a man again. Pray you, sit still. ) *He's fine again.*

L. MACBETH You have displaced the mirth, broke the good
meeting.   *Being serious.*
With most admired disorder.

MACBETH                      Can such things be, *represents*
*She seems* And overcome us like a (summer's cloud,) *peaceful*
*in control* Without our special wonder? You make me strange *nature.*
*Appearance* Even to the disposition that I owe,
*of* When now I think you can behold such sights. *Banquo's*
*reality* And keep the natural ruby of your cheeks, *ghost*
*(pretends)* When mine is blanched with fear.

ROSS            *Shows its only* (What sights, my lord?) 115
            *Macbeth who saw it*
L. MACBETH I pray you speak not (he grows worse and worse.)
*Protects* Question enrages him. (At once, good night.) *Tells them*
*MB* Stand not upon the order of your going.    *to leave.*
But go at once.

LENNOX               Good night, and better health

Attend his Majesty.
L. MACBETH   *Speaks for* (A kind good night to all.)    120
            *him*
[*Exeunt all but* MACBETH *and* LADY MACBETH

MACBETH   It will have blood, they say. Blood will have blood. *Scared*
(Stones have been known to move) and trees to speak.) *to*
*From* *get*
*Order & to Chaos.*    *Gravestones.*    ⑬ *caught*

The strain of the evening's events tells on Lady Macbeth. She is quiet. Macbeth intends to learn his future from the witches. He means to continue his bloody course.

**123**    **Augurs** These were diviners who, looking at the entrails of birds they had killed, gave indications of what the future might hold, or the 'truth' of what had already happened.

      **understood relations** the connections between events have been understood

**124**    **maggot-pies ... rooks** magpies, jackdaws and rooks

**124–5** **brought ... blood** have been used to reveal the most secret murderer

**125**    **What is the night?** What time of night is it?

**127–8** **How say'st ... bidding** What do you think of Macduff's refusal to come?

**131–2** **tomorrow, and betimes** early tomorrow morning

**133**    **bent ... worst** determined to learn the worst news by the worst means (witchcraft)

**134–5** **For mine ... way** All other matters must give way to my good

**135–7** **I am ... o'er** I am so far advanced on this murderous course that even if I were to go no further through this river of blood it would still be no easier to go back than to go on

**138**    **will to hand** must be done

**139**    **scanned** revealed, come to light

**140**    **season of all natures** power which preserves all life

**141**    **strange and self-abuse** strange self-deception

**142**    **Is the ... use** is the beginner's fear which lacks the toughness of experience

Hecate is angry with the witches.

**2**    **beldams** hags

**3**    **Saucy** Insolent

*Dark nature reveals truth?*

Augurs and understood relations have
By maggot-pies and choughs and rooks brought
    forth
The secret'st man of blood. What is the night?    125

L. MACBETH  (Almost at odds with morning, which is which.)  *She can't tell the difference*

MACBETH  How say'st thou that Macduff denies his person
At our great bidding?

L. MACBETH                          Did you send to him, sir?

MACBETH  I hear it by the way, but I will send.
There's not a one of them but in his house    130
I keep a servant fee'd. I will tomorrow,
And betimes I will, to (the weird sisters.)  *witches*
More shall they speak; for now I am bent to know
By the worst means, the worst. For mine own good,
All causes shall give way (I am in blood    *grim.*    135
Stepped in so far, that,) should I wade no more,
Returning were as tedious as go o'er.
Strange things I have in head, that will to hand,
Which must be acted ere they may be scanned.

L. MACBETH  You lack the season of all natures, sleep. )  *sleep → peace*
*They won't get any.*

MACBETH  Come, we'll to sleep. My strange and self-abuse
Is the initiate fear, that wants hard use.
(We are yet but young in deed.)

                                              [*Exeunt*

## Scene ❺

*Thunder. Enter the three* WITCHES *meeting* HECATE

1ST WITCH  Why how now Hecate? You look angerly.

HECATE  Have I not reason, beldams as you are.
Saucy, and overbold, how did you dare

115

Hecate makes it plain that the witches should not have dealt with Macbeth without her knowledge. Possibly they should not have dealt with Macbeth at all. She has further problems in mind for him. (Like the other witches scenes, most of this is written in shorter rhymed lines.)

| | | |
|---|---|---|
| 4 | **trade and traffic** | do business with |
| 7 | **close ... harms** | secret organiser of all damage done |
| 11 | **wayward** | awkward, perverse |
| 12 | **wrathful** | angry |
| 13 | **Loves ... for you** | his affections are selfish ones; they do not consider you |
| 15 | **pit of Acheron** | Hell (Acheron was one of the rivers in Hell.) |
| 18 | **vessels** | utensils, cauldrons |
| 20 | **I am for the air** | I shall rise into the air (Hecate is the moon goddess.) |
| 21 | **dismal ... end** | Hecate is planning Macbeth's future. |
| 22 | **wrought** | carried out |
| 24 | **vaporous drop profound** | drop of liquid of great significance |
| 26 | **distilled ... sleights** | concentrated by cunning and trickery |
| 27 | **artificial sprites** | supernatural beings created by witchcraft |
| 29 | **Shall ... confusion** | will lead him to destruction |
| 30–1 | **He shall ... fear** | He will be made to dismiss fate and fear of death, and set his hopes far too high |
| 32–3 | **security ... enemy** | confidence in personal safety is the main danger for the human being |
| 35 | **stays** | is waiting |

To trade and traffic with Macbeth
In riddles and affairs of death;      5
And I, the mistress of your charms,
The close contriver of all harms,
Was never called to bear my part,
Or show the glory of our art?
And, which is worse, all you have done      10
Hath been but for a wayward son,
Spiteful, and wrathful, who, as others do,
Loves for his own ends, not for you.
But make amends now: get you gone,
And at the pit of Acheron      15
Meet me i' th' morning. Thither he
Will come to know his destiny.
Your vessels and your spells provide,
Your charms, and every thing beside.
I am for the air; this night I'll spend      20
Unto a dismal and a fatal end.
Great business must be wrought ere noon.
Upon the corner of the moon
There hangs a vaporous drop profound.
I'll catch it ere it come to ground;      25
And that distilled by magic sleights,
Shall raise such artificial sprites,
As by the strength of their illusion,
Shall draw him on to his confusion.
He shall spurn fate, scorn death, and bear      30
His hopes 'bove wisdom, grace and fear;
And you all know security
Is mortals' chiefest enemy.
[*Music and a song within, 'Come away, come*
    *away,' etc.*
Hark! I am call'd; my little spirit, see,
Sits in a foggy cloud, and stays for me.      35

                          [*Exit*

**1st Witch**   Come, let's make haste! She'll soon be back again.

                          [*Exeunt*

With heavy irony, Lennox recalls recent events and Macbeth's reactions to them. The lord says that Malcolm has been welcomed at the English court.

**1–2**   **My former ... farther** You can draw your own conclusions from what I have already told you

**2**   **Only I say** I am just saying that

**3**   **borne** managed

**4–5**   **The gracious ... dead** Macbeth expressed his pity over the death of Duncan – granted, once he was dead

**5**   **Banquo ... late** Banquo took a walk in the dark

**6**   **Whom ... killed** And, if you like, Fleance killed him

**7**   **For Fleance fled** and the fact that Fleance escaped made him guilty

**8**   **Who cannot ... thought** Who can fail to think

**monstrous** unnatural

**10**   **Damned fact** A sinful deed

**11**   **How ... Macbeth!** Look how it grieved Macbeth!

**straight** immediately

**12**   **In pious rage** in righteous fury

**12–13**   **the two ... sleep** stab those two guards who were asleep on the job, drunk and fast asleep

**13**   **thralls** captives

**17**   **He has ... well** he has managed things well for himself

**17–20**   **I do ... Fleance** It's my opinion that if he had access to Duncan's sons, which, please God, he never will, they would discover what it means to kill a father; and so would Fleance

**19**   **an't** if it

**21**   **peace** enough of that

**from broad words** as a result of his outspokenness

**21–2**   **failed His presence** did not appear

**tyrant** the villain who rules as king

**24**   **he bestows himself** he lodges now

**25**   **holds ... birth** withholds his birthright (the crown)

## Scene 6

*Enter* LENNOX *and another* LORD → Represent
Scotland.

LENNOX    My former speeches have but hit your thoughts
Which can interpret farther. Only I say
Things have been strangely borne. The gracious Duncan
(Was pitied of Macbeth – marry he was dead.) was guilty
And the right-valiant Banquo walked too late. 5

Fled like Duncan's sons.
(Whom you may say, if't please you, Fleance killed,
For Fleance fled) – men must not walk too late,
Who cannot want the thought how monstrous
It was for Malcolm and for Donalbain
To kill their gracious father? Damned fact. It's a lie 10
How it did grieve Macbeth! Did he not straight
In pious rage the two delinquents tear,
That were the slaves of drink, and thralls of sleep?

Being Sarcastic Was not that nobly done? Ay, and wisely too;
's suspicious For 'twould have angered any heart alive 15
To hear the men deny 't. So that, I say equivocation
He has borne all things well; and I do think
That, had he Duncan's sons under his key –
As, an't please heaven, he shall not – they should find
What 'twere to kill a father. So should Fleance. 20

nobody can speak the truth in Scotland.
But peace – for from broad words, and 'cause he failed
His presence at the tyrant's feast, I hear
Macduff lives in disgrace. Sir, can you tell
Where he bestows himself?

LORD                   The son of Duncan,
From whom this tyrant holds the due of birth, 25
Lives in the English Court, and is received

The lord tells Lennox that Macduff has also gone to the English court to urge the king to provide an army so that Macbeth can be defeated and peace be returned to Scotland.

**27**    **most pious Edward** Edward the Confessor, King of England

**28–9**    **That the ... respect** Malcolm is still held in high regard, in spite of the cruel misfortune he has suffered.

**29–30**    **Thither ... King** Macduff has gone there to beg the holy King

**30**    **upon his aid** on his behalf

**31**    **wake Northumberland** call the Earl of Northumberland to arms

**32–3**    **with Him ... work** with God's help and approval of the war

**34–7**    **Give to ... now** We want to eat and sleep without fear, feast without the threat of murder, be loyal to the rightful king and know that there are no strings attached to any gift or honour we receive; we lack all this at the moment

**38**    **exasperate the King** annoyed King Edward

**39**    **Sent ... Macduff?** Did he send a message to Macduff? There is confusion between the two kings here in the text of the play. It seems to mean that Macbeth tried to get Macduff onside. He of course refused.

**40**    **with ... 'Sir, not I'** with an absolute refusal

**41**    **cloudy** sullen

    **me his back** his back on him

**42–3**    **hums ... answer'** mutters, as if to say 'You'll regret this answer you've laid on me'

**43**    **clogs** burdens

**44**    **to a caution** to be careful

**48–9**    **our ... accursed** country that is suffering, but is also under the rule of a murdering tyrant

Of the most pious Edward with such grace,
That the malevolence of fortune nothing
Takes from his high respect. Thither Macduff
Is gone to pray the holy King, upon his aid          30
To wake Northumberland, and warlike Siward,
That by the help of these, with Him above
To ratify the work, we may again
Give to our tables meat, sleep to our nights,
Free from our feasts and banquets bloody knives,     35
Do faithful homage, and receive free honours,
All which we pine for now. And this report
Hath so exasperate the King, that he
Prepares for some attempt of war.

LENNOX                              Sent he to Macduff?

LORD   He did; and with an absolute 'Sir, not I',     40
The cloudy messenger turns me his back,
And hums, as who should say, 'You'll rue the time
That clogs me with this answer.'

LENNOX                              And that well might
Advise him to a caution, to hold what distance
His wisdom can provide. Some holy angel            45
Fly to the Court of England, and unfold
His message ere he come, that a swift blessing
May soon return to this our suffering country
Under a hand accursed.

LORD                     I'll send my prayers with him.

[*Exeunt*

*Handwritten annotations:*

not geting food no sleep.

Macbeth

Macduff refuses
MB
He should take care

He can stay, but goes to fight.

poison, night, danger, fertility

# Act 3 scenes 3 to 6

## Filming scene 3

### Work in a group of five

1 You are going to write a screenplay for scene 3. The main difference between a theatre playscript and a film screenplay is that a screenplay describes the action in detail. It is also set out in a different way:

```
EXT. A PATH NEAR THE PALACE. NIGHT

1ST MURDERER and 2ND MURDERER are standing waiting.
Suddenly they hear a sound. Both look round startled.
3RD MURDERER appears from between some trees. They
stare at him.

            1ST MURDERER

      But who did bid thee join
      with us?
```

2 Cast the parts and read the scene through aloud.

3 Discuss how you imagine the scene will look.

4 Now each take one section of the scene to work on. The following sections have deliberately been chosen to overlap:
   - lines 1–8
   - lines 4–14
   - lines 8–15
   - lines 12–18
   - lines 15–22

### Work on your own

5 Write the screenplay for your section.

### Work in your group of five

6 Take it in turns to read out your screenplay and explain it to the others.

# Scene 4: Macbeth's moods

In this scene Macbeth experiences a rollercoaster of emotion. At the beginning of the scene he is playing the part of the King: noble, gracious, and welcoming. By the end of it he is preoccupied with his fears of what he has done and what he still has to do.

**Work on your own**

1 Read the scene through again, paying particular attention to Macbeth's speeches.

2 Copy this table:

| Lines | What Macbeth says | What it tells us |
|-------|-------------------|------------------|
| 1–2 | At first I And last the hearty welcome. | |
| 11 | There's blood upon thy face. | |
| 20 | | Suddenly he is worried: Fleance is alive and so he is still a threat. |
| 23–4 | | |
| 37–8 | | |
| 48 | | |
| 77–9 | | |
| 92 | | |
| 121 | | |
| 131–2 | | |
| 135–7 | | |

3 In the middle column, write the quotations against the line numbers.

4 For each quotation explain, in your own words, what you think this tells us about Macbeth's state of mind.

# Witches and a ghost

This section of the play has two different non-human characters: the ghost of Banquo, and Hecate. It also has the three witches, whom we have met before. All these characters present a theatre director with an interesting challenge.

## *Staging the ghost*

It is clear from seventeenth century documents that when *Macbeth* was first staged, Banquo's Ghost appeared physically on stage, even though only Macbeth can see him. Some modern productions make the ghost 'invisible' so that Macbeth and the audience have to imagine him.

### Work with a partner

1 Read Act 3 scene 4 lines 31–72 together. One of you should read the part of Macbeth while the other reads the other parts.

2 Discuss these questions:

    **a** How effective would this section be if the ghost was invisible?

    **b** If he is invisible, how can the audience be helped to 'see' him?

    **c** If he is visible, what should be look like?

    **d** What other effects could be used to make these lines effective:

        • lighting
        • sound effects
        • music
        • special effects?

3 Now work together to write a description of how you would stage this scene, including the second appearance of the ghost (lines 88–106). Write about 100 words.

# Plot summary quiz

The 12 short quotations below sum up the story of these scenes.

1 Work out the correct order for them.

2 Work out who said each one.

**A**

…at the pit of Acheron
Meet me i' th' morning…

**B**

And this report
Hath so exasperate the King, that he
Prepares for some attempt of war.

**C**

But now I am cabined, cribbed, confined, bound in
To saucy doubts and fears.

**D**

Hark! I hear horses.

**E**

I am in blood
Stepped in so far, that, should I wade no more,
Returning were as tedious as go o'er.

**F**

Pray you keep seat,
The fit is momentary…

**G**

Stand not upon the order of your going.
But go at once.

**H**

There's blood upon thy face.

**I**

There's but one down; the son is fled.

**J**

Thou canst not say I did it; never shake
Thy gory locks at me.

**K**

Which of you have done this?

**L**

Why do you make such faces? When all's done,
You look but on a stool.

125

The witches prepare the cauldron while they wait for Macbeth to arrive.

1  **brinded** brindled, streaked

2  **hedge-pig** hedgehog

3  **Harpier** A familiar spirit gives the signal to start.

7–8  **Days ... got** has sweated poison for a month and been captured in its sleep

10  **Double** Increase twofold (This also suggests deception – a double meaning.)

12  **Fillet ... snake** A strip of flesh taken from a marshland snake

16  **fork** forked tongue

**blind-worm** slow-worm (not a snake but a legless lizard once believed, wrongly, to be poisonous)

17  **owlet** a little owl

23  **Witches' mummy** medicine prepared from a witch's corpse

**maw and gulf** stomach and gut

24  **ravined** gorged, glutted

25  **Root of hemlock** A common poisonous plant in our hedgerows.

**digged i' th' dark** dug up at night (for full poisonous effect)

# Act Four

## Scene ❶

*Macbeth gets referred to using dark animous.*

*Thunder. Enter the three* WITCHES

| | |
|---|---|
| 1ST WITCH | Thrice the brinded cat hath mewed. |
| 2ND WITCH | Thrice and once the hedge-pig whined. |
| 3RD WITCH | Harpier cries ''Tis time, 'Tis time.' |

1ST WITCH     Round about the cauldron go,
In the poisoned entrails throw.     5
Toad, that under cold stone
Days and nights hast thirty-one
Sweltered venom sleeping got,
Boil thou first i' th' charmed pot.

ALL     Double, double toil and trouble;     10
Fire burn, and cauldron bubble.

2ND WITCH     Fillet of a fenny snake,
In the cauldron boil and bake.
Eye of newt, and toe of frog,
Wool of bat, and tongue of dog,     15
Adder's fork, and blind-worm's sting,
Lizard's leg, and owlet's wing,
For a charm of powerful trouble,
Like a hell-broth boil and bubble.

ALL     Double, double toil and trouble;     20
Fire burn, and cauldron bubble.

3RD WITCH     Scale of dragon, tooth of wolf,
Witches' mummy, maw and gulf
Of the ravined salt-sea shark,
Root of hemlock digged i' th' dark,     25
Liver of blaspheming Jew,     *go to hell*

Hecate comes to check that all is ready. The witches dance to seal the charm. Hecate leaves and Macbeth arrives, commanding the witches to tell him what he wants to know.

27    **Gall** A bitter substance found in the gall bladder.

      **slips of yew** cuttings from the yew tree (often grown in churchyards and considered poisonous)

28    **Slivered** sliced off

      **moon's eclipse** a time of ill-omen

29    **Turk, and Tartar** infidels (and in Shakespeare's time, people noted for their cruelty)

30    **birth-strangled** strangled at birth (Such a child would not have been baptised and so would never be able to go to Heaven.)

31    **Ditch-delivered ... drab** born in a ditch of a prostitute

32    **slab** sludge

33    **chaudron** guts

SD    *three other Witches* These are not the original three. These will sing and dance a chorus.

47    **secret** mysterious, occult

      **black ... hags** witches who practise black magic

48    **without a name** nameless, too horrible to give a name

49    **I conjure ... profess** I entreat you, by the witchcraft which you claim

52    **yesty** foaming

53    **Confound ... navigation up** wreck and sink shipping

Gall of goat, and slips of yew
Slivered in the moon's eclipse,
Nose of Turk, and Tartar's lips,
Finger of birth-strangled babe    *Dead baby*    30
Ditch-delivered by a drab,    *Born from a whore in*
Make the gruel thick and slab.    *a ditch.*
Add thereto a tiger's chaudron,
For th' ingredients of our cauldron.

ALL        Double, double toil and trouble;        35
           Fire burn, and cauldron bubble.

2ND WITCH  Cool it with a baboon's blood,
           Then the charm is firm and good.

           *Enter* HECATE *with three other Witches*

HECATE     O well done! I commend your pains,
           And every one shall share i' th' gains.        40
           And now about the cauldron sing,
           Like elves and fairies in a ring,
           Enchanting all that you put in.

                    [*Music and song, 'Black spirits', etc.*

                                    [*Exit* HECATE

2ND WITCH  By the pricking of my thumbs,
           Something wicked this way comes:        45

                            [*Knock within*

           Open, locks, whoever knocks.

           *Enter* MACBETH

MACBETH    How now, you secret, black and midnight hags!
           What is't you do?

ALL                    A deed without a name.    *isn't natural*
                                               *↳ supernatural*
MACBETH    I conjure you by that which you profess,    *Order*
           Howe'er you come to know it, answer me.        50
           Though you untie the winds and let them fight    *evil vs good.*
           Against the churches; though the yesty waves
           Confound and swallow navigation up;

The First Apparition appears from the cauldron. It is a helmeted head, and it warns Macbeth to be cautious of Macduff.

54      **bladed ... lodged** unripe corn be blown flat

56      **slope** lean

57–8    **though ... together** though the precious seeds from which all living things come are thrown into disorder

59      **till destruction sicken** until destruction gets sick of destroying

62      **our masters** i.e. those who command the witches and who will take the form of apparitions

64      **farrow** piglets a sow has just delivered

        **sweaten** sweated

65      **gibbet** scaffold

SD      ***an armed head*** a head wearing a helmet

73      **harped** touched on

75      **potent** powerful

Though bladed corn be lodged, and trees blown
    down;
Though castles topple on their warders' heads;) FS  55
Though palaces and pyramids do slope
Their heads to their foundations; though the
    treasure
Of nature's germens tumble all together,
Even till destruction sicken; answer me
To what I ask you.

**1ST WITCH**                                   Speak.

**2ND WITCH**                                Demand.

**3RD WITCH**                                        We'll answer.   60

**1ST WITCH**   Say if thou'dst rather hear it from our mouths,
Or from our masters?)

**MACBETH**                        Call 'em, let me see 'em.

**1ST WITCH**   Pour in sow's blood, that hath eaten
Her nine farrow; grease that's sweaten
From the murderer's gibbet throw                    65
Into the flame.

**ALL**                       Come high or low;)
Thyself and office deftly show.

*Thunder.* 1ST APPARITION: *an armed head*)

**MACBETH**   Tell me, thou unknown power –

**1ST WITCH**                        He knows thy thought.
Hear his speech, but say thou nought.

**1ST APP.**   Macbeth, Macbeth, Macbeth) beware Macduff;   70
Beware the Thane of Fife. Dismiss me. Enough.

[*Descends*

**MACBETH**   Whate'er thou art, for thy good caution thanks;
Thou hast harped my fear aright. But one word
    more –

**1ST WITCH**   He will not be commanded. Here's another,
More potent than the first.                         75

*Handwritten annotations:*
his castle gets overrun.
evil, shows Macbeth is evil
bc. he can hear the evil master
call their masters.
a warrior. Macbeth's head FS
3 times
Macbeth
He can't command the evil.

131

The Second Apparition tells Macbeth that no man born of woman can harm him. The Third Apparition says that he will not be defeated until Birnham Wood moves to Dunsinane. Macbeth is filled with confidence.

**SD**    *a bloody child* a child covered in blood

**82**    **yet I'll ... sure** I have had assurances about the future but I'll make doubly certain

**83**    **take ... fate** compel fate to fulfil its promise

          **Thou ... live** To make sure of his own safety, he will kill Macduff.

**84–5**  **That ... thunder** so that I can prove my cowardly fears to be groundless, and I shall be able to sleep, even through thunder

**86**    **issue** child

**87–8**  **round ... sovereignty** royal crown

**89**    **Be lion-mettled** Take on yourself the spirit of the lion

**89–90** **take ... conspirers are** do not concern yourself about people who are raging, discontented or may be conspiring against you

**94**    **impress the forest** enlist trees into their service

**95**    **Sweet bodements, good!** Prophecies that promise well!

**98**    **live ... nature** live out his natural life

**99**    **mortal custom** natural death

**101**   **issue** descendants

**102**   **in this kingdom** Macbeth's last hope is that Banquo's descendants might reign elsewhere.

*Thunder.* 2ND APPARITION: *a bloody child*

*[handwritten: F.S. the Child he'll kill.]*

2ND APP.    Macbeth, Macbeth, Macbeth!

*[handwritten: 3 times]*

MACBETH    Had I three ears, I'd hear thee.

2ND APP.    Be bloody, *bold* and resolute; laugh to scorn

*[handwritten: brave]*

The power of man, for none of woman born
Shall harm Macbeth.

*[handwritten: He is immortal]*

80

*[handwritten: Changes his mind.]*                    [*Descends*

MACBETH    Then live, Macduff – what need I fear of thee?
But yet I'll make assurance double sure,
And take a bond of fate. Thou shalt not live;
That I may tell pale-hearted fear it lies,
And sleep in spite of thunder.

*Thunder.* 3RD APPARITION: *a child crowned, with
a tree in his hand*

*[handwritten: Child of King. Malcolm - leanage]*

What is this,                    85
That rises like the issue of a king,
And wears upon his baby brow the round
And top of sovereignty?

ALL                              Listen, but speak not to 't.

*[handwritten: He's a snake now]*

3RD APP.    Be lion-mettled, proud and take no care
Who chafes, who frets, or where conspirers are.    90
Macbeth shall never vanquished be, until
Great Birnam wood to high Dunsinane hill
Shall come against him.

                              [*Descends*

MACBETH                    That will never be.
Who can impress the forest, bid the tree
Unfix his earth-bound root? Sweet bodements,
    good!                                              95

*[handwritten: Banquo's ghost. Macbeth's guilt.]*

Rebellious dead, rise never till the wood
Of Birnam rise, and our high-placed Macbeth
Shall live the lease of nature, pay his breath
To time and mortal custom. Yet my heart
Throbs to know one thing. Tell me, if your art    100
Can tell so much, shall Banquo's issue ever
Reign in this kingdom?

133

At Macbeth's insistence the witches conjure up a 'show' of eight kings, indicating that Banquo's descendants will indeed be crowned. Macbeth is totally dejected.

**105**    **noise** music

**110**    **shadows** images

         **so** in the same way

**SD**    ***A show of eight kings*** Eight is the correct number of Stuart kings, omitting Mary Queen of Scots, James Stuart's mother, who was beheaded by Queen Elizabeth I, the monarch immediately before James I.

**SD**    ***glass*** mirror

**112**    **sear** burn

**115**    **Start, eyes!** Eyes, jump from your sockets!

**116**    **crack of doom** trumpet blast of Judgement Day

**120**    **twofold ... sceptres** The Scottish coronation used one orb and one sceptre; the English, one orb and two sceptres. This is a tribute to James, indicating that his descendants would inherit the throne which he had united. He was James VI of Scotland, James I of England.

**122**    **blood-boltered** Banquo's hair is matted with blood.

**126**    **sprites** spirits

**129**    **antic round** bizarre circular dance

**130**    **great King** Macbeth (and a reference to James I)

**131**    **Our duties ... pay** the respects we paid him made him welcome

| | |
|---|---|
| ALL | Seek to know no more. |
| MACBETH | I will be satisfied. Deny me this, |
| | And an eternal curse fall on you. Let me know. |

[*Oboes*

Why sinks that cauldron, and what noise is this?  105

| | |
|---|---|
| 1ST WITCH | Show! |
| 2ND WITCH | Show! *} 3 times* |
| 3RD WITCH | Show! |
| ALL | Show his eyes, and grieve his heart; |
| | Come like shadows, so depart.  110 |

*A show of eight kings, the last with a glass in
his hand;* BANQUO *following*   James I sees himself.

| | |
|---|---|
| MACBETH | Thou art too like the spirit of Banquo. Down! |
| | Thy crown does sear mine eye-balls; and thy hair, |
| | Thou other gold-bound brow, is like the first. |
| | A third is like the former. Filthy hags, |
| | Why do you show me this? – A fourth? Start, eyes!  115 |
| | What, will the line stretch out to th' crack of doom? |
| | Another yet? A seventh? I'll see no more. |

He sees the king

| | |
|---|---|
| | And yet the eighth appears, who bears a glass, |
| | Which shows me many more; and some I see |
| | That twofold balls and treble sceptres carry.  120 |
| | Horrible sight! Now I see 'tis true, |
| | For the blood-boltered Banquo smiles upon me, |
| | And points at them for his. What, is this so? |

[*Exeunt kings and* BANQUO

| | |
|---|---|
| 1ST WITCH | Ay, sir, all this is so. But why |
| | Stands Macbeth thus amazedly?  125 |
| | Come sisters, cheer we up his sprites, |
| | And show the best of our delights. |
| | I'll charm the air to give a sound, |
| | While you perform your antic round; |
| | That this great King may kindly say,  130 |
| | Our duties did his welcome pay. |

[*Music. The* WITCHES *dance, and vanish*

135

Macbeth tells Lennox to come in. He has not seen the witches and they did not go past him. His news is that the riders Macbeth heard have brought news. Macduff has gone to England. This immediately marks him as an enemy. Macbeth intends to seize Macduff's castle and slaughter his family.

**132**   **pernicious** ruinous

**133**   **aye** forever

**134**   **without there** whoever that is outside

**138**   **And damned ... them** and may all who put their trust in them also be damned; this is an example of **irony** (see Glossary p. 241), since Macbeth has put his trust in them throughout.

**143**   **Time ... exploits** Time, you have forestalled my terrible deeds

**144–5**   **The flighty ... with it** Intentions arrived at quickly will never be carried out unless the action is equally swift

**146–7**   **The very ... hand** my very first intended plans from now on shall be the first deeds I carry out

**148**   **be it ... done** let it be no sooner thought than done

**150**   **give to ... sword** cut down

**151–2**   **souls ... line** every member of his family, however distantly related

**154**   **no more sights** let's have no more apparitions

MACBETH     Where are they? Gone? Let this pernicious hour
            Stand aye accursed in the calendar.
            Come in, without there!

            *Enter* LENNOX

LENNOX                          (What's your Grace's will?)

MACBETH     Saw you the weird sisters?

LENNOX                          No, my lord.                    135
                                            2, supernatural
MACBETH     Came they not by you?                    Do they
                                                            exist?
LENNOX                          No indeed, my lord.

MACBETH     Infected be the air whereon they ride,
            And damned all those that trust them. I did hear
            The galloping of horse. Who was't came by?

LENNOX      'Tis two or three, my lord, that bring you word     140
            (Macduff is fled to England.) on a mission.

MACBETH                          Fled to England?

LENNOX      Ay my good lord.

MACBETH     Time, thou anticipat'st my dread exploits.
            The flighty purpose never is o'ertook
            Unless the deed go with it. From this moment        145
            The very firstlings of my heart shall be
            The firstlings of my hand. And even now,
            To crown my thoughts with acts, be it thought
              and done.
            The castle of Macduff I will surprise,

Kill        Seize upon Fife, give to the edge o' th' sword      150
everyone.   His wife, his babes, and all unfortunate souls
            That trace him in his line. No boasting like a fool;
Hacks       This deed I'll do before this purpose cool.
lineage.    But no more sights! Where are these gentlemen?
            Come bring me where they are.                       155

Malcolm, Duncan                          [*Exeunt*
Fleance, Banquo

# Act 4 scene 1

## Casting the spell

The opening of this scene is the part of *Macbeth* that everyone remembers: three witches around a cauldron, chanting :

*Double, double toil and trouble;*
*Fire burn, and cauldron bubble.*

There are two problems with lines like these. Firstly they are so well known that people tend not to think about what they actually mean. And because they are so well known, it's easy to find them funny.

However, in Shakespeare's time, many people *did* believe in witches, and found them evil and terrifying. So how do we get that idea across today?

**Work in a group of four**

1  You're going to work together on lines 1–38. Begin by casting the parts. The fourth person will be the director.

2  Each read through the lines silently. As you read:

   **a**  try to hear the sounds and rhythms of the words

   **b**  get a picture in your mind of the things they are describing

   **c**  think about how all three of the witches move and behave.

3  Now read the lines aloud, without movement, using the sounds and rhythms to express the pictures the words describe. The director should listen carefully, and think of ways the reading can be improved.

4  Discuss how you can perform this scene. In particular think about:

   **a**  what each speaker does as she speaks

   **b**  how the others react and move: do they remain silent, or do they make any sounds? Do they stay still, or do they move?

5  Now try the lines again, putting your ideas into practice.

   **a**  Did your performance bring out the evil and menace of the witches?

   **b**  How could you develop it further?

# Questions and answers

Macbeth went to meet the witches to find out their answers to questions that had been disturbing him.

**Work with a partner**

1 Read aloud lines 60–99, with one of you reading Macbeth's lines, and the other all the rest.

2 At the beginning, Macbeth wants to ask one or more questions but never gets the chance. But each of the three apparitions gives him an answer to a question he might have asked. Take a large sheet of paper and copy this diagram:

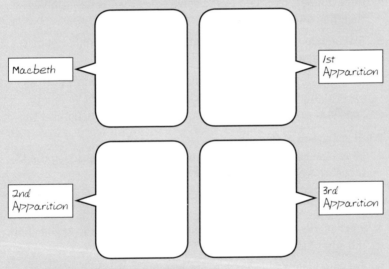

(If you like, you can replace the named boxes with your own drawings of the characters.)

3 In each of the apparition speech balloons, sum up in a few words the information that Macbeth is given.

4 In Macbeth's speech balloon, write down what you think his question (or questions) might have been.

# A show of eight kings

If every character appearing in this scene were played by a different actor, you would need 18 actors to play:

- three witches
- Hecate
- Macbeth
- three apparitions
- eight kings
- Banquo
- Lennox

No theatre company today could afford the wages! So a director needs to think of creative ways of presenting the apparitions and the Kings. Here are some ideas:

- huge puppets operated by the stage crew wearing dark clothes so that they cannot be seen

- film or video projected in screens hanging down in different places on the stage

- Macbeth close to the audience and lit so that we concentrate on his face. Behind him and further away there is a light show with special effects and music. We 'see' everything in Macbeth's face.

**Work in a group of four**

1   Read again the lines in which the apparitions appear (68–93) and those where Macbeth sees the kings (111–23).

2   You have been given the job of directing this scene in a modern theatre. You only have enough actors to play the parts of the witches, Hecate, Macbeth, and Ross. Discuss how you would show the apparitions and the kings.

3   For your planned production, produce the following documents:

   a   a paragraph each explaining how you will present:
       - the apparitions
       - the show of eight kings.

   b   a picture showing how one of the apparitions will appear

   c   a picture showing how the show of eight kings will appear

   d   a set of notes listing the sound effects and music you will use.

## Quotation quiz

The 11 short quotations below all come from this scene.

1 Work out the correct order for them.

2 Work out who said each one.

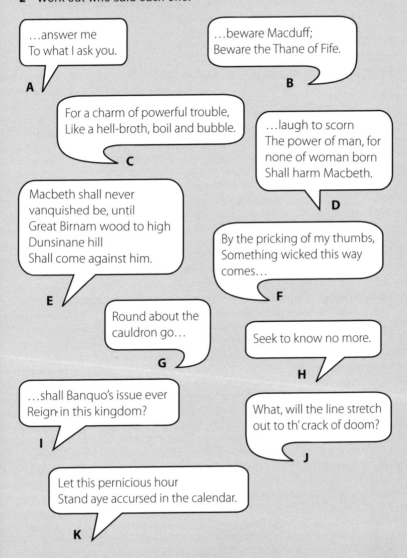

…answer me
To what I ask you.

**A**

…beware Macduff;
Beware the Thane of Fife.

**B**

For a charm of powerful trouble,
Like a hell-broth, boil and bubble.

**C**

…laugh to scorn
The power of man, for
none of woman born
Shall harm Macbeth.

**D**

Macbeth shall never
vanquished be, until
Great Birnam wood to high
Dunsinane hill
Shall come against him.

**E**

By the pricking of my thumbs,
Something wicked this way
comes…

**F**

Round about the
cauldron go…

**G**

Seek to know no more.

**H**

…shall Banquo's issue ever
Reign in this kingdom?

**I**

What, will the line stretch
out to th' crack of doom?

**J**

Let this pernicious hour
Stand aye accursed in the calendar.

**K**

Ross has told Lady Macduff about her husband's flight to England. Lady Macduff condemns Macduff's selfishness in running away – as she sees it – at such a dangerous time.

| | |
|---|---|
| **3–4** | **When our ... traitors** He has not been disloyal to Macbeth, but the fear which has caused him to flee makes him look guilty |
| **7** | **his titles** his rank and his possessions |
| **9** | **he wants ... touch** he lacks the natural instincts |
| | **poor** feeble |
| **10** | **The most diminutive** the very smallest |
| **12** | **fear** (for himself) |
| | **love** (for his family) |
| **14** | **coz** cousin (This can literally be the family relationship or just a close friendship.) |
| **15** | **school** control |
| **17** | **fits o' th' season** conditions of the time |
| **19** | **do not know ourselves** are deeply confused (because our loyalties are divided between our love of our country and our duty to the crowned king) |
| **19–22** | **when we hold ... move** rumour works on our fears without our knowing what we do fear; it's like being cast adrift on a stormy sea which buffets us to and fro |
| **24** | **Things ... upward** When things are at their worst that is either the end, or the beginning of an improvement |
| **25** | **pretty** fine |

## Scene 2

*Cute child*

*Enter* LADY MACDUFF, *her* SON, *and* ROSS

L. MACDUFF    What had he done, to make him fly the land?

ROSS    You must have patience, madam.

L. MACDUFF                                    He had none. *He left her, not patient.*

His flight was madness. When our actions do not,
Our fears do make us traitors.

ROSS                                    You know not
Whether it was his wisdom, or his fear.                    5

L. MACDUFF    Wisdom! to leave his wife, to leave his babes,

*His family is dead*

His mansion, and his titles in a place
From whence himself does fly(He loves us not;)
He wants the natural touch, for the poor wren,
The most diminutive of birds, will fight,                    10
Her young ones in her nest,(against the owl.) *Macbeth*
All is the fear, and nothing is the love;                    *critter of the*
As little is the wisdom, where the flight                    *night.*
So runs against all reason.

ROSS                                    My dearest coz,

I pray you school yourself. But for your husband,    15
He is noble, wise, judicious, and best knows
The fits o' th' season.(I dare not speak much
further,) *Because its a secret mision*
But cruel are the times, when we are traitors,
And do not know ourselves; when we hold
      rumour
From what we fear, yet know not what we fear,    20
But float upon a wild and violent sea
Each way and move. I take my leave of you;
Shall not be long but I'll be here again.

*gona get better or worse*

Things at the worst will cease, or else climb
      upward
To what they were before. My pretty cousin,    25

Ross leaves, and Lady Macduff and her son show a shared, loving relationship in their conversation.

29    **It would ... discomfort** I would weep and you would be embarrassed

30    **Sirrah** A term of address used by parents to children, as well as by masters to servants.

      **dead** we shall not see him again (meaning he might as well be dead)

34-5  **thou'dst ... gin** you are too innocent to fear bird traps

34    **lime** bird-lime (a sticky substance spread on twigs to catch birds)

35    **pitfall** fowler's snare

      **gin** trap

36    **Poor ... for** Traps are not intended to catch wretched birds

42-3  **with wit ... thee** you are bright for your age

47    **swears, and lies** breaks an oath of allegiance

Blessing upon you!

L. MACDUFF Fathered he is, and yet he's fatherless. *Her son → poor boi*

ROSS I am so much a fool, should I stay longer,
It would be my disgrace and your discomfort.
I take my leave at once.

[*Exit*

L. MACDUFF *Dead to her.* (Sirrah, your father's dead) 30
And what will you do now? How will you live?

SON As birds do, mother.

L. MACDUFF What, with worms, and flies?

SON With what I get I mean, and so do they.

L. MACDUFF Poor bird, thou'dst never fear the net nor lime,
The pitfall nor the gin. 35

SON Why should I, mother? Poor birds they are not set for.
My father is not dead for all your saying.

L. MACDUFF Yes, he is dead. How wilt thou do for a father?

SON Nay, how will you do for a husband?

L. MACDUFF Why, I can buy me twenty at any market. 40

SON Then you'll buy 'em to sell again.

L. MACDUFF Thou speakest with all thy wit, and yet, i' faith with
wit enough for thee.

SON Was my father a traitor, mother? *Qt*

L. MACDUFF Ay, that he was. 45

SON What is a traitor?

L. MACDUFF Why one that swears, and lies. }

SON And be all traitors that do so?

L. MACDUFF Every one that does so is a traitor, and must
be hanged. *K.* 50

SON And must they all be hanged that swear and lie?

L. MACDUFF Every one.

SON Who must hang them?

L. MACDUFF Why, the honest men.

A messenger arrives to warn Lady Macduff that danger threatens. There is nowhere she can go to escape. She hesitates, but the murderers are already there.

| | |
|---|---|
| **63** | **Poor prattler** Poor little chatterer |
| **65** | **in your ... perfect** I am perfectly aware of your high rank |
| **66** | **doubt** fear |
| | **nearly** closely |
| **67** | **homely** lowly |
| **70–1** | **To do ... person** not to warn you would be an act of fiercest cruelty, and fiercest cruelty is too close to you |
| **75** | **laudable** praiseworthy |
| | **sometime** sometimes |
| **76** | **Accounted ... folly** reckoned to be dangerous foolishness |
| **78** | **What ... faces?** Why are you looking like that? |
| **80** | **unsanctified** unholy |
| **82** | **shag-eared** shaggy hair over the ears |

SON     Then the liars and swearers are fools, for there are  55
liars and swearers enough to beat the honest men,
and hang up them.

*Clever kid?*

L. MACDUFF   Now God help thee, poor monkey! But how wilt
thou do for a father?

SON     If he were dead, you'd weep for him. If you  60
would not, it were a good sign that I should
quickly have a new father.

*He knows he not dead.*

L. MACDUFF   Poor prattler, how thou talk'st!

*Enter a* MESSENGER

MESSENGER   Bless you fair dame. I am not to you known,
Though in your state of honour I am perfect.  65
I doubt some danger does approach you nearly.
If you will take a homely man's advice,
Be not found here. Hence with your little ones!
To fright you thus, methinks I am too savage;
To do worse to you were fell cruelty,  70
Which is too nigh your person. Heaven preserve you,
I dare abide no longer.

*Tells her to leave*

*Might be Lennox in disguise*

                                        [*Exit*

L. MACDUFF                Whither should I fly?
I have done no harm. But I remember now
I am in this earthly world, where to do harm
Is often laudable, to do good sometime  75
Accounted dangerous folly. Why then, alas,
Do I put up that womanly defence,
To say I have done no harm?

*Enter* MURDERERS

                            What are these faces?

1ST M.     Where is your husband?  *Reminds us he's not there*

L. MACDUFF   I hope in no place so unsanctified  80
Where such as thou may'st find him.

1ST M.                           He's a traitor.

SON     Thou liest thou shag-eared villain.

*Brave*

147

Her son is killed, and Lady Macduff runs away, chased by the murderers.

**82**   **egg** baby

**83**   **Young ... treachery** Offspring of a traitor

Macduff is at the English court seeking Malcolm's help, but Malcolm is a little suspicious of him. He finds ways to examine his loyalty.

**2**   **bosoms** hearts

**3**   **Hold fast** grip tightly

   **mortal** deadly

**4**   **Bestride** stand over, defend

   **our down-fallen birthdom** our native land, which has been laid low

**4–5**   **Each ... cry** The audience knows, but Macduff does not, that his wife and children have been killed. This an example of **dramatic irony** (see Glossary p. 239).

**6**   **that it resounds** so that heaven echoes

**7**   **felt** suffered

**8**   **Like ... dolour** the same cry of grief

   **wail** mourn for

**9**   **redress** put right

**10**   **As** when

   **to friend** favourable

**11**   **perchance** perhaps

**12**   **sole name** name alone

**13**   **honest** honourable

   **loved him well** served him loyally

**14**   **He hath ... yet** he has not done anything to you yet

**14–17**   **but something ... god** you may have observed something of Macbeth in me, and think it wise to offer me up as a sacrifice to an angry god

1ST M.                    What, you egg! *Insult*

                             [*Stabs him*

Young fry of treachery!

SON                    He has killed me, mother:

Run away, I pray you! *To show he's dead Tries to protect her.* [*Dies*

           [*Exit* LADY MACDUFF, *crying 'Murder!',*
                  *and pursued by the murderers*

*From drama to a subdue mood.*

## Scene ❸

*Enter* MALCOLM *and* MACDUFF    *D.I*      *Could be*

MALCOLM    Let us seek out some desolate shade, and there *comenting*
*grieve*      Weep our sad bosoms empty.        *on whom just*

MACDUFF                    Let us rather *happened.*

*fight.*    Hold fast the mortal sword, and like good men,

          Bestride our down-fallen birthdom. Each new morn,

   *D.I*    (New widows howl, new orphans cry,) new sorrows    5

*his fam*   Strike heaven on the face, that it resounds

   *is dead* As if it felt with Scotland, and yelled out

          Like syllable of dolour.

MALCOLM              What I believe, I'll wail;

          What know, believe; and what (I can redress,) *wants to*
          As I shall find the time to friend, I will.      *make things*   10
          What you have spoke, it may be so perchance. *better.*

*recognizes*    This tyrant, whose sole name blisters our tongues,
*appearance*   Was once thought honest;) you have loved him well;
*of reality.*   He hath not touched you yet. I am young, but something

*you might*   You may deserve of him through me, and wisdom   15
*here to*      To offer up a weak, poor, innocent lamb
*betray*      T' appease an angry god.
*me"*

MACDUFF   I am not treacherous.

*doesnt trust Macduff*

149

Macduff is dismayed at Malcolm's attitude to him, and fears for Scotland's future. Malcolm appreciates Macduff's love of his country. However to test him he warns him that Scotland might be worse off when Macbeth is removed from power and he is king himself.

**19–20** **may recoil ... charge** might give way if a king commands

**20–1** **But I ... transpose** But I must demand your pardon. My thoughts cannot change the man that you are

**22** **though ... fell** though it was the brightest one that fell (Satan or Lucifer was the brightest angel in heaven until he rebelled against God and was cast out.)

**23–4** **Though all ... so** Though all that is evil would like to put on a good appearance, it doesn't alter the fact that what is good still looks good

**24–5** **I have ... doubts** Macduff's hope is gone, but Malcolm says that perhaps his hopes were dashed for the same reason that Malcolm has to be suspicious.

**26–28** **Why in ... leave-taking?** Why did you leave your wife and children without saying goodbye? Why did you abandon those whom you love and leave them undefended? Malcolm is concerned that this might prove that Macduff had done some kind of deal with Macbeth.

**27** **precious motives** dear reasons for existing

**29–30** **Let not ... safeties** do not let my suspicions discredit you, they are for my self-protection

**30** **rightly just** perfectly honourable

**32** **lay ... sure** make sure you have a really sound basis

**33–4** **Wear ... affeered** You can be perfectly open about your crimes, your title is confirmed

**title** 1) claim to the throne 2) tyranny

**37** **to boot** as well, in addition

**42** **in my right** to support my rightful claim

**43** **gracious England** the King of England, Edward the Confessor

**45** **tread ... head** i.e. one way of killing a snake

**46** **wear ... sword** show off his head on the point of my sword

MALCOLM                         But Macbeth is.

A good and virtuous nature may recoil
In an imperial charge. But I shall crave your
     pardon.                                20

*evil things with good appearance*

That which you are, my thoughts cannot transpose:
Angels are bright still, though the brightest fell.
Though all things foul would wear the brows of
     grace,
Yet grace must still look so.

*appearance of reality*

MACDUFF                            I have lost my hopes.

MALCOLM     Perchance even there where I did find my doubts.   25

Why in that rawness left you wife and child,
Those precious motives, those strong knots of love,
Without leave-taking? I pray you,
Let not my jealousies be your dishonours,
But mine own safeties. You may be rightly just,      30
Whatever I shall think.

*we watch a man suffer*

MACDUFF                     Bleed, bleed, poor country;

Great tyranny, lay thou thy basis sure,
For goodness dare not check thee. Wear thou thy
     wrongs,      *Affirmed*
The title is affeered. Fare thee well, lord;
I would not be the villain that thou think'st      35
For the whole space that's in the tyrant's grasp,
And the rich East to boot.

*Reflects Scotland as a 'fear country'*

MALCOLM                      Be not offended;

I speak not as in absolute fear of you.
I think our country sinks beneath the yoke;
It weeps, it bleeds, and each new day a gash      40
Is added to her wounds. I think withal,
There would be hands uplifted in my right;
And here from gracious England have I offer
Of goodly thousands. But, for all this,
When I shall tread upon the tyrant's head,      45
Or wear it on my sword, yet my poor country
Shall have more vices than it had before,

*Slavery of Macbeth.*

*new atrocities (D.I) Macduff doesn't know*

*wants to end a revolution*

*Deceives Macduff to see how loyal he is*

*Macduff is a traitor to his family not to his country*

Malcolm says that when he comes to the throne the people of Scotland will want Macbeth back. He says that his lust knows no bounds, and that Scotland's wives and daughters will not be safe from him. Macduff is surprised, but assures him that it need not be a problem.

**48**   **sundry** various

**49**   **By him** through him

**What should he be?** Who can you be talking about?

**51**   **grafted** implanted

**52**   **opened** revealed

**55**   **confineless harms** limitless evils

**legions** ranks, army

**57**   **top** surpass

**57–9** **grant ... malicious** admit that he is bloodthirsty, lustful, greedy, dishonourable, lying, violent, evil

**59**   **smacking** full

**61**   **voluptuousness** lust

**Your** Scotland's

**63**   **cistern** pit, pool

**64**   **All continent ... o'erbear** would overcome all restraining forces

**65**   **will** lust

**66–7** **Boundless ... tyranny** Uncontrollable appetites can take hold of the whole nature and control it; this is tyranny

**70**   **take upon ... yours** accept the kingship, succeed to the throne

**71**   **Convey ... plenty** manage your pleasures in secrecy, as much as you like

**72**   **The time ... hoodwink** You can fool the world in this way

**74**   **vulture** ravenous appetite

**74–6** **devour ... inclined** cope with all that number who will offer themselves to a king when he so desires

**77**   **ill-composed affection** unbalanced temperament

**78**   **staunchless avarice** greed that cannot be satisfied

More suffer, and more sundry ways, than ever,
By him that shall succeed.

MACDUFF                                    What should he be?

MALCOLM     It is myself I mean; in whom I know          50
All the particulars of vice so grafted,
That when they shall be opened, black Macbeth
Will seem as pure as snow, and the poor state
Esteem him as a lamb, being compared
With my confineless harms.

MACDUFF                              Not in the legions     55
Of horrid hell can come a devil more damned
In evils, to top Macbeth.

MALCOLM        Macbeth is:     I grant him bloody,
Luxurious, avaricious, false, deceitful,
Sudden, malicious, smacking of every sin
That has a name. But there's no bottom, none,      60
In my voluptuousness. Your wives, your daughters,
Your matrons, and your maids, could not fill up
The cistern of my lust, and my desire
All continent impediments would o'erbear,
That did oppose my will. Better Macbeth              65
Than such a one to reign.

MACDUFF                                Boundless intemperance
In nature is a tyranny; it hath been
Th' untimely emptying of the happy throne,
And fall of many kings. But fear not yet
To take upon you what is yours: you may              70
Convey your pleasures in a spacious plenty,
And yet seem cold. The time you may so hoodwink.
We have willing dames enough. There cannot be
That vulture in you, to devour so many
As will to greatness dedicate themselves,            75
Finding it so inclined.

MALCOLM                            With this, there grows
In my most ill-composed affection, such
A staunchless avarice, that were I King,

*handwritten margin notes:* "I'll do worse than Macbeth"; violent; lustful; lust; moderation; to moderation; doom; vice; plies to Macbeth

Macduff is more concerned about Malcolm's self-confessed greed, but he says that, too, can be overcome. However, when Malcolm claims that he has no kingly qualities at all, Macduff is in utter despair.

| | |
|---|---|
| 79 | **cut off** kill |
| 80 | **his** that man's |
| 82 | **forge** make up |
| 85–6 | **Sticks ... lust** is more deeply embedded, more dangerously rooted than lust, which is much more short-lived |
| 87 | **the sword ... kings** the reason for the death of Scottish kings who have been murdered |
| 88 | **foisons** abundant supplies |
| 89 | **Of your mere own** that already belong to you |
| | **these are portable** these faults are bearable |
| 90 | **With ... weighed** balanced against your other qualities |
| 91 | **king-becoming graces** qualities which a king should have |
| 92 | **verity** truth |
| | **temp'rance** moderation |
| 93 | **Bounty** generosity |
| 94 | **fortitude** reliability |
| 95–6 | **I have ... crime** I have no trace of any of them, but have plenty of variations on every sort of evil |
| 97–100 | **had I ... earth** if I held power I would destroy harmony, turn peace everywhere into commotion, and disrupt all agreement on earth |
| 100 | **O Scotland, Scotland!** Macduff here addresses his speech to Scotland as if the country were a person (for **personification** see Glossary p. 241). The direct address – often prefaced by 'O' – is called **apostrophe** (see Glossary p. 238). |
| 104 | **untitled** usurping, not king by right |
| 106–8 | **Since ... breed** since the most legitimate, the truest heir to your throne, has ruled himself out and stands accursed, dishonouring his own parentage |
| 111 | **Died ... lived** lived each day holily, as if it were to be her last |

I should cut off the nobles for their lands,
Desire his jewels and this other's house,　　80
And my more-having would be as a sauce
To make me hunger more, that I should forge
Quarrels unjust against the good and loyal,
Destroying them for wealth.

MACDUFF　　　　　　　　　　This avarice
Sticks deeper, grows with more pernicious root　　85
Than summer-seeing lust; and it hath been
The sword of our slain kings; yet do not fear;
Scotland hath foisons to fill up your will,
Of your mere own. All these are portable,
With other graces weighed.　　　　　　90

MALCOLM　But I have none. The king-becoming graces,
As justice, verity, temp'rance, stableness
Bounty, perseverance, mercy, lowliness,
Devotion, patience, courage, fortitude,
I have no relish of them, but abound　　95
In the division of each several crime,
Acting it many ways. Nay, had I power, I should
Pour the sweet milk of concord into hell,
Uproar the universal peace, confound
All unity on earth.

MACDUFF　　　　　　O Scotland, Scotland!　　100

MALCOLM　If such a one be fit to govern, speak.
I am as I have spoken.

MACDUFF　　　　　　　Fit to govern?
No, not to live. O nation miserable,
With an untitled tyrant bloody-sceptered,
When shalt thou see thy wholesome days again,　　105
Since that the truest issue of thy throne
By his own interdiction stands accursed,
And does blaspheme his breed? Thy royal father
Was a most sainted King; the Queen that bore thee,
Oftener upon her knees than on her feet,　　110
Died every day she lived. Fare thee well,

*[Handwritten annotations: "what happens to Macbeth.", "generosity", "Macbeth has nothing of this.", "What a good king should have", "Dispair", "Crowned himself.", "Macbeth", "lineage", "praying", "lived as if it was her last day."]*

155

Macduff's reaction convinces Malcolm of his sincerity. Malcolm confesses that what he has said about himself is completely untrue, and merely a test of Macduff's loyalty. An army has been raised to fight Macbeth. Macduff is confused by this turn of events.

**112–13** **These evils ... Scotland** the evils which you recite against yourself are the very same evils which Macbeth has, and they have driven me from Scotland

**115** **Child of integrity** which comes from honesty

**116** **black scruples** dark suspicions

**118** **trains** plots

**119–20** **modest ... haste** ordinary common sense warns me about being too quick to believe everything I am told

**122** **to thy direction** in your hands

**123–5** **Unspeak ... nature** withdraw what I said against myself and renounce the vices I confessed, as foreign to my character

**125–6** **I am ... woman** I have had no relations with women

**never was forsworn** was never deceitful

**127** **Scarcely ... mine own** hardly coveted what was in fact already my own

**coveted** desired

**133–5** **Whither ... forth** and indeed to that country, before your arrival, the Earl of Northumberland, with an army of 10,000 men, fully prepared, was setting off

**133** **here-approach** arrival

**134** **Old Siward** Earl of Northumberland

**135** **at a point** fully prepared

**136–7** **the chance ... quarrel** may our chance of success be as sure as the justice of our cause

**138** **at once** at one and the same time

**139** **reconcile** accept, take in

**140** **King** (Edward the Confessor)

**142** **stay his cure** wait to be cured by him (King Edward was said to have powers of healing.)

**malady** illness

**142–3** **convinces ... art** defeats the efforts of medical science

*He won't support Malcolm.*

These evils thou repeat'st upon thyself
Hath banished me from Scotland. O my breast –
Thy hope ends here.

MALCOLM                                Macduff, this noble passion,
Child of integrity, hath from my soul          115
Wiped the black scruples, reconciled my thoughts
To thy good truth and honour. Devilish Macbeth

*has tricked him*

By many of these trains hath sought to win me
Into his power; and modest wisdom plucks me
From over-credulous haste; but God above          120
Deal between thee and me. For even now
I put myself to thy direction, and
Unspeak mine own detraction; here abjure
The taints and blames I laid upon myself,          *I was lying*
For strangers to my nature. I am yet          125

*Virgin* — Unknown to woman, never was forsworn,
Scarcely have coveted what was mine own,

*He wouldn't betray anyone* — At no time broke my faith, would not betray
The devil to his fellow, and delight
No less in truth than life. My first false speaking          130
Was this upon myself. What I am truly,
Is thine, and my poor country's, to command;
Whither indeed, before thy here-approach,
Old Siward, with ten thousand warlike men
Already at a point, was setting forth.          135
Now we'll together, and the chance of goodness
Be like our warranted quarrel. Why are you silent?          *Because he's heard good news.*

MACDUFF          Such welcome and unwelcome things at once
'Tis hard to reconcile.

*Enter a* DOCTOR          *figure of trust*

MALCOLM          Well, more anon. Comes the King forth, I pray
you?          140

DOCTOR          Ay, sir, there are a crew of wretched souls
That stay his cure. Their malady convinces

Malcolm explains the English king's powers of healing. Ross arrives with news from Scotland.

| | |
|---|---|
| **145** | **presently amend** are cured instantly |
| **146** | **the evil** scrofula, or the king's evil (a disease in which swollen glands break through the skin) |
| **148** | **here-remain** stay |
| **149** | **solicits heaven** gets help from heaven |
| **150** | **strangely-visited** extraordinarily afflicted |
| **152** | **mere** complete |
| **153** | **stamp** coin |
| **154** | **'tis spoken** it is said |
| **156** | **healing benediction** blessed gift of healing |
| | **virtue** power |
| **158** | **sundry** various |
| **159** | **grace** divine grace |
| **160** | **I know him not** 1) I do not recognise him 2) I do not know if he is friend or foe |
| **162** | **I know him now** I know who he is now |
| **162–3** | **betimes ... strangers!** quickly remove the obstacles which make strangers of us! |
| **164** | **Stands ... did?** Are things in Scotland the same as they were before? |
| **166–7** | **where nothing ... smile** where only someone who knows nothing about the situation can ever smile |
| **168** | **rend** pierce |

The great assay of art; but at his touch,
Such sanctity hath Heaven given his hand,
They presently amend.

MALCOLM                          I thank you doctor.          145

                                    [*Exit* DOCTOR

MACDUFF    What's the disease he means?

MALCOLM                              'Tis called the evil:
A most miraculous work in this good King,
Which often since my here-remain in England
I have seen him do. How he solicits heaven,
Himself best knows; but strangely-visited people,   150
All swollen and ulcerous, pitiful to the eye,
The mere despair of surgery, he cures,
Hanging a golden stamp about their necks,
Put on with holy prayers; and 'tis spoken,
To the succeeding royalty he leaves          155

*wonderful*
*King.*        The healing benediction. With this strange virtue,
He hath a heavenly gift of prophecy,
And sundry blessings hang about his throne,
That speak him full of grace.

*Enter* ROSS

MACDUFF                          See, who comes here?

MALCOLM    My countryman; but yet I know him not. *Doesnt*          160
                                                    *trust him.*

MACDUFF    My ever-gentle cousin, welcome hither.

MALCOLM    I know him now. Good God, betimes remove
The means that makes us strangers!

ROSS                                  Sir, amen.

MACDUFF    Stands Scotland where it did?

ROSS  &      *Appearance of reality*  Alas, poor country!
*Foul/*      Almost afraid to know itself. It cannot          165
*Fair*       Be called our mother, but our grave; where nothing
But who knows nothing is once seen to smile;
Where sighs, and groans, and shrieks that rend the
    air,          *softening*

Ross's news is of a Scotland suffering under Macbeth's evil control. Macduff asks Ross about Lady Macduff and his children, but Ross is evasive to begin with.

**169**    **not marked** not noticed

**170**    **modern ecstasy** common feeling

**170–1**    **The dead ... who** People hardly bother asking for whom the funeral bell is ringing

**173**    **or ere they sicken** even before they get ill

**173–4**    **relation too nice** the story is too detailed

**174**    **newest** latest

**175**    **That of ... speaker** The person who tells of something which happened an hour previously is criticised because the news is already old

**176**    **teems** gives birth to

**179**    **well at peace** 1) thriving 2) dead (Ross is delaying giving the full horror of the news straight away and so uses two possible meanings. He is answering Macduff's question about the present state of Scotland.)

**180**    **Be not ... speech** Don't be a miser with your words

**181–2**    **the tidings ... borne** the news which has been a great weight to bear

**183**    **were out** had left home

**185**    **For that** because

        **power afoot** army preparing

**186**    **your eye** if you were seen

**188**    **doff** throw off

**189**    **England** the King of England

**192**    **gives out** reports

**192–3**    **Would ... like** I wish I could answer this comforting news with something similar

**193–4**    **words ... would be** words which ought to be

**195**    **latch** catch

*every day feels violent*

Are made, not marked; where violent sorrow seems
(A modern ecstasy.) The dead man's knell                    170
Is there scarce asked for who, and good men's lives
Expire before the flowers in their caps,) *war*
Dying or ere they sicken.

MACDUFF                                             O relation
Too nice and yet too true!

MALCOLM                                        What's the newest grief?

ROSS          That of an hour's age doth hiss the speaker.        175
Each minute teems a new one.

MACDUFF            *She's in heaven* How does my wife?

ROSS          Why, well. — *equivocation*          *Tension*

MACDUFF                    And all my children?

ROSS                                              Well too.

MACDUFF      The tyrant has not battered at their peace?

ROSS          No, they were well at peace, when I did leave 'em.

MACDUFF      Be not a niggard of your speech. How goes 't?        180

ROSS          When I came hither to transport the tidings,
*Bad news* (Which I have heavily borne,) there ran a rumour
Of many worthy fellows that were out;
Which was to my belief witnessed the rather,
For that I saw the tyrant's power afoot.                    185
Now is the time of help; your eye in Scotland
Would create soldiers, make our women fight,
To doff their dire distresses.

MALCOLM                          Be 't their comfort *to please*
We are coming thither. (Gracious England) hath *king James*
Lent us good Siward, and ten thousand men;        *190  I*
An older and a better soldier none
That Christendom gives out.

ROSS                              Would I could answer
This comfort with the like. But I have words
That would be howled out in the desert air,
Where hearing should not latch them.

Ross gives Macduff the news of the murder of his whole family. Macduff is stunned and seems unable to understand that it can have happened. Malcolm urges him to be angry and talk of revenge.

**196**      **The general cause** Relating to everyone

**196–7**      **fee-grief ... breast** sorrow concerning one particular person

**199**      **Pertains to** concerns

**202**      **possess** inform

**205**      **To relate the manner** To tell you how it was done

**206**      **quarry ... deer** 1) deer 2) dear ones – a **play on words** (see Glossary p. 242)

           **quarry** the heap of dead bodies when deer have been hunted and killed

**210**      **Whispers ... heart** whispers to the over-burdened heart

**212**      **must be from thence** had to be away from there

**214–15**      **Let's ... grief** Let us create medicine out of our great revenge; to do the same to Macbeth will cure our mortal grief

**216**      **He has no children** 1) Macbeth has no children and so a similar revenge cannot be taken 2) Malcolm has no children and in making this suggestion shows he cannot understand how I feel

**217**      **hell-kite** bird of prey from hell

**218**      **dam** mother

**219**      **one fell swoop** one cruel attack; the swift downward death strike by a bird of prey. Shakespeare's use of this phrase in *Macbeth* has since become a **proverb** (see Glossary p. 242).

MACDUFF            What concern they? 195
The general cause? Or is it a fee-grief
Due to some single breast? *One person*

ROSS            No mind that's honest
But in it shares some woe; though the main part
Pertains to you alone.

MACDUFF        If it be mine,  *Act quickly*
Keep it not from me, quickly let me have it. *like Macbeth*
                  200

ROSS  Let not your ears despise my tongue for ever,
Which shall possess them with the heaviest sound
That ever yet they heard.

MACDUFF         Hum! I guess at it.

ROSS  Your castle is surprised; your wife and babes
Savagely slaughtered. To relate the manner,    205
Were on the quarry of these murdered deer
To add the death of you. *It'd kill you too*

MALCOLM        Merciful heaven!
What! man; ne'er pull your hat upon your brows,
Give sorrow words; the grief that does not speak
Whispers the o'er-fraught heart, and bids it break. 210

MACDUFF  My children too?

ROSS        Wife, children, servants all
That could be found. *no men. Attacked the weak.*

MACDUFF       And I must be from thence!
My wife killed too?

ROSS       I have said.

MALCOLM           Be comforted.
Let's make us medicines of our great revenge,
To cure this deadly grief. *wants fight, loyalty and* 215
           *his country*

MACDUFF  He has no children. All my pretty ones?
Did you say all? O hell-kite! All? *animal imagery to*
What, all my pretty chickens and their dam *makes us see*
At one fell swoop?       *Macbeth as evil*

*Macduff experiences an internal turmoil*

Macduff blames himself for his family's deaths. He promises to settle his score personally with Macbeth when they meet on the battlefield. They leave to join up with the English forces and march to Scotland.

| | | |
|---|---|---|
| 220 | **Dispute it** | Fight against it |
| 224 | **take their part** | act on their behalf |
| 225 | **They were ... thee** | they were all slaughtered because of you |
| | **Naught** | Evil |
| 226 | **demerits** | faults |
| 228 | **whetstone** | sharpening stone |
| 229 | **Convert** | change |
| | **blunt ... enrage it** | be angry, not depressed |
| 231 | **braggart** | boaster |
| 232 | **intermission** | delay |
| | **Front to front** | Face to face |
| 235 | **Heaven ... too** | may God have mercy on his soul |
| | **tune** | way of speaking |
| 236 | **Come ... the King** | Come, let us go to the King (King Edward) |
| | **power** | army |
| 237 | **Our ... leave** | All we need to do is to take our leave |
| 238 | **ripe for shaking** | ready to be shaken down |
| | **the powers above** | angels, good spirits |
| 239 | **Put ... instruments** | arm themselves |
| | **cheer** | comfort |

MALCOLM   Dispute it like a man.

MACDUFF                              I shall do so;                    220
          But I must also feel it as a man:
          I cannot but remember such things were

*Wife &*
*Kids.*
          (That were most precious to me) Did heaven look
              on,                                    GUILT
          And would not take their part? (Sinful Macduff,)
          They were all struck for thee. Naught that I am,   225

*internal*
*turmoil.*
          Not for their own demerits, but for mine,
          Fell slaughter on their souls. Heaven rest them
              now.                                Uses his

MALCOLM   Be this the whetstone of your sword. Let grief  grief
*manipulate*   Convert to anger: blunt not the heart, enrage it.

MACDUFF   O I could play the woman with mine eyes,) Cry   230
          And braggart with my tongue! But gentle heavens,
          Cut short all intermission. Front to front
          Bring thou this fiend of Scotland and myself;
          (Within my sword's length set him, If he 'scape,
          Heaven forgive him too.) Wants to fight.

MALCOLM                              This tune goes manly.   235
          Come go we to the King. Our power is ready,
          Our lack is nothing but our leave. Macbeth

*Fruit*
*↓*
*growth*
          Is <u>ripe</u> for shaking, and the powers above
          Put on their instruments. Receive what cheer you
              may,
*↓*
*ready to*
*fight.*
          The night is long that never <u>finds the day.</u> FS    240

              Macbeth's          MB dies      [*Exeunt*
                 rule                        great uplift.

# Act 4 scenes 2 and 3

## Performance: scene 2

This scene ends horrifyingly – with a small child being murdered on stage. Shakespeare prepares for this horror by giving us a conversation between the boy and his mother. The better this is performed, the more horrifying the end of the scene will appear.

### Work with a partner

1  Each read silently lines 30–63.

2  Cast the two parts, and read the lines aloud.

3  Now look at the list of prompts below. They suggest different ways in which the characters might be played. Each choose one for your character and think about how it will affect your performance of the scene.

4  Now read the lines, following your chosen prompt.

5  When you have finished, discuss how the scene went. Then choose different prompts and try the scene again.

### Prompts:

| Lady Macduff | Son |
| --- | --- |
| Angry and bitter at her husband, but trying to conceal her feelings from her son. | Concerned at the way his mother is behaving, and trying to cheer her up. |
| Sad and a bit depressed – she's hardly got the energy to answer all these questions her son keeps asking. | Irritable that his mother is behaving the way she is – why can't she just snap out of it? |
| Strong and determined. Although she has become a single parent, she has the courage and determination to keep going. | Wishing that his father had taken him with him. But now he's the 'man' of the house, he must look after his mother. |

# Character: Macduff

We learn a lot about Macduff in these two scenes. Although he doesn't actually appear in scene 2, we learn what his wife thinks of his behaviour, and we make our own judgements based on what he has done.

**Work on your own**

1 Make a list of at least five words that describe Macduff's character based on these two scenes. You can choose your own words, or you can select from the list below.
   **Warning:** the list contains a number of words that are probably not suitable to describe Macduff.

| | | | |
|---|---|---|---|
| brave | cowardly | cunning | depressed |
| easily taken in | far-sighted | foolish | honest |
| honourable | hopeless | loyal | patriotic |
| selfish | shrewd | treacherous | weak |

2 For each of the words you have chosen find some evidence to support your choice. This may be:
   - something Macduff says
   - something he does
   - something someone else says about him.

3 Copy the table below and use it to record your ideas. Write the words in the 'Point' column.

4 Use the 'Explanation' column to link the word you have chosen and the evidence you have found.

5 The table has been started for you. You should choose five words in addition to the one that appears in the table.

| Point | Evidence | Explanation |
|---|---|---|
| easily taken in | Fit to govern? No not to live. | Malcolm has been pretending that he is a wicked man who cannot control his lust. Macduff believes he is telling the truth, rather than just testing him out. |
| | | |

# Themes: good/evil, weak/strong

*Macbeth* is a play that explores the theme of good versus evil. In Acts 1 to 3 we see how Macbeth moves from being a brave national hero to a wicked murderer. All ideas of goodness seem to vanish from the play. However, at the end of the story, good triumphs over evil, and it is in Act 4 that we begin to see the return of good.

**Work in a small group**

1 Take a large sheet of paper and copy the diagram below. It contains a matrix on which you can place the characters at the end of scene 3. As you can see, one character has been drawn in already.

2 Place each of the following characters on the matrix, according to where you think they are at this point in the play:

Macbeth    Lady Macbeth    Malcolm    Macduff    Ross

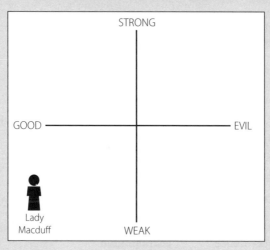

3 For each character, find a suitable quotation either by them or about them. Write it next to that character on the diagram, like this:

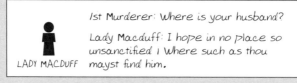

# Quotation quiz

For each of these quotations, work out:

1 who said it
2 who they were speaking to
3 what it tells us about
   a the speaker
   b the situation
   c any other characters.

**A**
Alas, poor country!
Almost afraid to know
itself. It cannot
Be called our mother,
but our grave…

**B**
Front to front
Bring thou this fiend of Scotland
and myself;
Within my sword's length set him…

**C**
His flight was madness. When
our actions do not,
Our fears do make us traitors.

**D**
I am in this earthly world,
where to do harm
Is often laudable, to do good
sometime
Accounted dangerous folly.

**E**
I think our country sinks
beneath the yoke;
It weeps, it bleeds…

**F**
If such a one be fit to govern, speak.
I am as I have spoken.

**G**
Let us seek out some desolate
shade, and there
Weep our sad bosoms empty.

**H**
Was my father a
traitor, mother?

**I**
What I am truly,
Is thine, and my poor
country's, to command…

**J**
What, all my pretty
chickens and their dam
At one fell swoop?

169

Lady Macbeth's lady-in-waiting has called a doctor to watch her mistress's sleepwalking. For two nights Lady Macbeth has not stirred, but now she enters, carrying a candle.

| | |
|---|---|
| **1** | **watched** waited up and observed |
| **4** | **field** battlefield |
| **5** | **nightgown** dressing-gown |
| **6** | **closet** a cabinet or chest for papers |
| **9** | **perturbation in nature** disturbance in her well-being |
| **10–11** | **effects of watching** things she would do when awake |
| **11** | **slumbery agitation** activity whilst asleep |
| **12** | **actual performances** acts |
| **14** | **I will not** I absolutely refuse to |
| **15** | **meet** proper |
| **18** | **her very guise** the exact way she appears |
| **20** | **close** hidden |

# Act Five

*L. Macbeth*

## Scene 1

*Enter a* DOCTOR *of* PHYSIC *and a* WAITING
GENTLEWOMAN   *represents trust*

DOCTOR   I have two nights watched with you, but can
perceive no truth in your report. When was it
she last walked?   *refers to Macbeth's battle*

GENTLEWOMAN   Since his Majesty went into the field, I have seen
her rise from her bed, throw her nightgown upon   5
her, unlock her closet, take forth paper, fold it,
write upon't, read it, afterwards seal it, and again
return to bed; yet all this while in a most fast sleep.

*represents common voice of Scotland*

*Glamis murdered sleep.*

DOCTOR   A great perturbation in nature, to receive at once
the benefit of sleep, and do the effects of   10
watching. In this slumbery agitation, besides her
walking, and other actual performances, what at
any time have you heard her say?

GENTLEWOMAN   That sir, which I will not report after her.

DOCTOR   You may to me; and 'tis most meet you should.   15

GENTLEWOMAN   Neither to you nor any one, having no witness
to confirm my speech.

*Enter* LADY MACBETH *with a taper*   *sets the scene*

*Sleepwalk*
*↳ Supernatural*

Lo you, here she comes. This is her very guise, and
upon my life, fast asleep. *change that happened*
Observe her, stand close. *in Macbeth.*   20

DOCTOR   How came she by that light?

GENTLEWOMAN   Why it stood by her. She has light by her
continually,'tis her command.

*○ Initially wants darkness*

Lady Macbeth rubs her hands together as though hoping to wash them clean, and then she begins speaking. The doctor is alarmed by what he hears: references to the deaths of Duncan and Lady Macduff, and – unknown to him – the death of Banquo.

**25**    **sense is shut** she cannot see

**31**    **Yet** Even now after all this washing

       **spot** stain

**32**    **set down** write down

**33**    **satisfy my remembrance** make me sure of what I have remembered

**46**    **Go to, go to!** Come away! (The Doctor is speaking to the Gentlewoman who has heard things that she should not have.)

**51**    **Oh! oh! oh!** This is possibly one long sigh.

**52**    **sorely charged** painfully burdened

**53–4**  **I would ... body** I wouldn't want such a heart in my breast for the sake of my whole body

**54**    **dignity** worth

DOCTOR You see her eyes are open. *[explain to the audience sleepwalking supernatural]*

GENTLEWOMAN Ay but their sense is shut. 25

DOCTOR What is it she does now? Look how she rubs her hands. *[washing blood from her hands.]*

GENTLEWOMAN It is an accustomed action with her, to seem
thus washing her hands. I have known her
continue in this a quarter of an hour. 30

L. MACBETH Yet here's a spot. *[Blood.]*

DOCTOR Hark! she speaks. I will set down what comes
from her, to satisfy my remembrance the more
strongly.

L. MACBETH Out damned spot, out I say! One, two; why 35
then 'tis time to do 't. Hell is murky. Fie my lord,
fie! A soldier, and afeard? What need we fear
who knows it, when none can call our power to
account? Yet who would have thought the old
man to have had so much blood in him? 40

*[her signal — thinks of what she's done.]*

*[ringing of the bell]*

DOCTOR Do you mark that? *[guilt / lineage.]*

L. MACBETH The Thane of Fife had a wife; where is she now?
What, will these hands ne'er be clean? No more
o' that my lord, no more o' that you mar all with
this starting. *[remembering the last time she was strong — Banquet.]* 45

*[She knows]*

*[Important because they died and now she's miserable]*

DOCTOR Go to, go to! You have known what you should not.

GENTLEWOMAN She has spoke what she should not, I am sure
of that. Heaven knows what she has known.

L. MACBETH Here's the smell of the blood still; all the perfumes
of Arabia will not sweeten this little hand. 50
Oh, oh, oh! *[emotion.]*

DOCTOR What a sigh is there! The heart is sorely charged.

GENTLEWOMAN I would not have such a heart in my bosom for
the dignity of the whole body.

DOCTOR Well, well, well. 55

GENTLEWOMAN Pray God it be sir.

*1, 111, 52*

The doctor says that Lady Macbeth needs a priest rather than a doctor. He warns the gentlewoman to keep an eye on her mistress. She must make sure that she has no means of harming herself.

| | |
|---|---|
| **57** | **practice** medical skill |
| **62** | **out on's** out of his |
| **63** | **Even so?** What? There's more? |
| **69** | **Directly** Immediately |
| **70** | **Foul ... abroad** Rumours of evil are widespread |
| **71** | **infected** corrupted |
| **73** | **More ... divine** She has more need of a priest |
| **75** | **means of all annoyance** all means of injuring herself |
| **76** | **still** constantly |
| **77** | **mated, and amazed** baffled and bewildered |

Scottish forces are gathering to join up with the English army, led by Macduff, Malcolm, and Siward.

| | |
|---|---|
| **1** | **power** army |

*some sleepwalkers → go to heaven*

DOCTOR
This disease is beyond my practice. Yet I have
known those which have walked in their sleep
who have died holily in their beds.

L. MACBETH
Wash your hands, put on your night-gown,          60
look not so pale. I tell you yet again Banquo's
buried; he cannot come out on's grave.

*she takes control*

DOCTOR
Even so?

L. MACBETH
To bed, to bed; there's knocking at the gate.
Come, come, come, come, give me your hand.     65
What's done cannot be undone. To bed, to bed,
to bed.
[*Exit*

*no*

*protective to Macbeth or her child ↓ before ambition took her over*

DOCTOR
Will she go now to bed?

GENTLEWOMAN Directly.

DOCTOR
Foul whisperings are abroad. Unnatural deeds     70
Do breed unnatural troubles; infected minds
To their deaf pillows will discharge their secrets.
More needs she the divine than the physician.
God, God forgive us all. Look after her,
Remove from her the means of all annoyance,     75
And still keep eyes upon her. So, good night.
My mind she has mated, and amazed my sight.
I think, but dare not speak.

*poisonous ideas*

*he knows she's ill*

*she may take her own life*

GENTLEWOMAN Good night, good doctor.

*last time we see her wracked with guilt*

[*Exeunt*

## Scene 2

*war*

*Enter, with drums and colours,* MENTEITH, CAITHNESS,
ANGUS, LENNOX, *and soldiers*

MENTEITH
The English power is near, led on by Malcolm,
His uncle Siward, and the good Macduff.

By this time Macbeth is almost without support. Only mercenaries stand with him. The Scots move on to Birnam to meet Malcolm's forces.

| | | |
|---|---|---|
| 3 | **Revenges** | Desire for revenge |
| | **dear causes** | deeply-felt reasons for revenge |
| 4–5 | **to the ... man** | rouse the dead to respond to the call to arms |
| 6 | **well** | probably |
| 8 | **file** | list |
| 10 | **unrough** | unshaved (because not old enough to shave) |
| 11 | **Protest ... manhood** | show for the first time that they are grown men, in battle for the first time |
| 15–16 | **cannot ... rule** | 1) he cannot control his frenzied behaviour 2) he cannot prevent his subjects from rebelling against this corruption |
| 18 | **Now ... faith-breach** | Now every minute desertions denounce his treason |
| 19 | **move ... command** | obey only because they are ordered to |
| 23 | **pestered** | troubled |
| 24–5 | **all that ... there** | all aspects of his own nature revolt against him |
| 26 | **where ... owed** | i.e. to Malcolm |
| 27 | **medicine** | cure |
| | **sickly weal** | sick land, commonwealth |
| 28–9 | **pour ... us** | we will shed every drop of blood to purify our country |
| 30 | **dew** | water |
| | **sovereign flower** | royal flower |

*Reason for revenge*

Revenges burn in them; for their dear causes
Would to the bleeding and the grim alarm
Excite the mortified man.  *where they meet Malcolm.*

ANGUS                    (Near Birnam wood)          5
Shall we well meet them; that way are they coming.

CAITHNESS   Who knows if Donalbain be with his brother?

LENNOX      For certain sir, he is not. I have a file
            Of all the gentry. There is (Siward's son,)
*not been*  And many unrough youths, that even now     10
*in battle* Protest their first of manhood.

MENTEITH                            What does the tyrant?

CAITHNESS   Great Dunsinane he strongly fortifies.
*mad or*    Some say he's mad; others, that lesser hate him,
*full of*   Do call it valiant fury; but for certain,
*fury*      He cannot buckle his distempered cause    15
            Within the belt of rule.

ANGUS       *not secret*        Now does he feel
            His secret murders sticking on his hands.
            Now minutely revolts upbraid his faith-breach.
*nobody*    Those he commands move only in command,
*respects*  (Nothing in love.) Now does he feel his title   20
*him.*      Hang loose about him (like a giant's robe *Macbeth will never fit in*
            Upon a dwarfish thief.) *Duncan's place.*

MENTEITH                     Who then shall blame
            His pestered senses to recoil and start,
            When all that is within him does condemn
            Itself for being there?

CAITHNESS                    Well, march we on,          25
            To give obedience where 'tis truly owed.
            Meet we the medicine of the sickly weal,
            And with him pour we, in our country's purge,
            Each drop of us.

LENNOX           *Malcolm*      Or so much as it needs,
            To dew the sovereign (flower,) and drown (the weeds.) 30
            Make we our march towards Birnam. *Macbeth.*
                                    [*Exeunt, marching*

177

Macbeth is extremely agitated. He is loudly confident of success because of what the apparitions have said, but his violent scorn towards the servant shows that he is ill-at-ease.

| | |
|---|---|
| **1** | **let them fly all** let all my thanes desert me |
| **3** | **taint** be weakened |
| **4–5** | **The spirits ... consequences** The apparitions which know the fates of all mortals |
| **8** | **epicures** pleasure-seeking weaklings |
| **9** | **The mind I sway by** The mind which governs me, which makes my thoughts go to and fro |
| **10** | **sag** droop |
| **11** | **The devil ... black** Go to the devil! |
| | **cream-faced loon** pasty-faced fool |
| **12** | **goose look** white and shaking |
| **14** | **over-red thy fear** paint your face with blood to hide your fear |
| **15** | **lily-livered** cowardly |
| | **patch** clown (A clown's make-up starts with a white face.) |
| **16** | **Death of thy soul** Your spirit has died |
| | **linen** A hard-wearing fabric made from flax, prized when it is bleached white. |
| **17** | **Are counsellors to fear** make other men afraid |
| | **whey-face** Whey is a colourless liquid left after milk has been made into cheese. |
| **19** | **sick at heart** really low, depressed |
| **20** | **When I behold –** Macbeth breaks off here. He has seen a terrified servant, he knows the army is near, and there must soon be an end to all this. |
| | **push** attack |

## Scene 3

*Enter* MACBETH, DOCTOR, *and attendants*

MACBETH    Bring me no more reports, let them fly all.
Till Birnam wood remove to Dunsinane,
I cannot taint with fear. What's the boy Malcolm?
Was he not born of woman? The spirits that know
All mortal consequences have pronounced me
   thus:                                                          5
'Fear not Macbeth, no man that's born of woman
Shall e'er have power upon thee.' Then fly false
   thanes,
And mingle with the English epicures.
The mind I sway by, and the heart I bear,
Shall never sag with doubt, nor shake with fear.    10

*Enter a* SERVANT

The devil damn thee black, thou cream-faced loon.
Where gott'st thou that goose look?

SERVANT    There is ten thousand –

MACBETH                              Geese, villain?

SERVANT                                          Soldiers sir.

MACBETH    Go prick thy face, and over-red thy fear,
Thou lily-livered boy. What soldiers, patch?      15
Death of thy soul, those linen cheeks of thine
Are counsellors to fear. What soldiers, whey-face?

SERVANT    The English force, so please you.

MACBETH    Take thy face hence.

                                    [*Exit* SERVANT
               Seyton! – I am sick at heart,
When I behold – Seyton, I say! – This push        20

*Handwritten annotations:*
- *Is a leader*
- *Questions him, sees fear in him*
- *Betrayed by thanes who are true to Scotland*
- *Afraid*
- *not scared*
- *Insults him, his manliness.*
- *White*
- *Goodness.*
- *Fear*

Macbeth feels old but he realises that he will never have what he might originally have expected of old age. He has no friends and his false rank has brought him worse than nothing. Suddenly his mood swings. He will fight to the death. The doctor tells him that Lady Macbeth's sickness is not a medical condition.

**21**    **cheer me ever** 1) hearten me forever 2) confirm me on the throne; this possible **play on words** looks at 'cheer' as 'chair' (see Glossary p. 242).

    **disseat me now** dethrone me at once and remove me from my present way of life

**23**    **sear** dry, withered state

**26**    **in their stead** in place of them

**27**    **mouth-honour** lip-service

    **breath** mere air

**28**    **would fain deny** would gladly withhold

**35**    **more horses** more horsemen

    **skirr ... round** thoroughly scour through the whole countryside

**37**    **your patient** Lady Macbeth

    **Not so sick** It is not so much that she is sick

**38**    **As ... fancies** but that she is troubled with relentless delusions

**40**    **minister to** treat

**41**    **rooted** firmly established

**42**    **Raze ... brain** rub out the troubles imprinted on the mind

**43**    **sweet oblivious antidote** welcome antidote to bring forgetfulness

**44**    **stuffed bosom** overburdened heart

    **perilous stuff** dangerous poison

**45–6**    **Therein ... himself** The only person who can achieve a cure is the patient herself

**47**    **physic** medicine

    **I'll none of it** I'll have nothing to do with it

*[Annotation left margin: battle that will decide everything]*

Will cheer me ever, or disseat me now. *[annotation: tired of]*
I have lived long enough. My way of life *[annotation: life]*
Is fallen into the sear, the yellow leaf; *[annotation: growth imagery]*
And that which should accompany old age,
As honour, love, obedience, troops of friends *[annotation: dying]*
I must not look to have; but in their stead
Curses, not loud but deep, mouth-honour, breath
Which the poor heart would fain deny, and dare not.
Seyton! *[annotation: Rather be dead]*

*[Annotation left margin: things he doesn't have]* *[annotation: reminds audience of where he is/where he was]*

*Enter* SEYTON

SEYTON    What's your gracious pleasure?

MACBETH                                What news more?    30

SEYTON    All is confirmed my lord, which was reported.

MACBETH   I'll fight, till from my bones my flesh be hacked.
          Give me my armour. *[annotation: wants to fight - old MB]*

SEYTON                        'Tis not needed yet.

MACBETH   I'll put it on. *[annotation: To feel safe, power and honour]*
          Send out more horses, skirr the country round,    35
          Hang those that talk of fear. Give me mine armour. *[annotation: to identify]*
          How does your patient, doctor? *[annotation: Lady MB]*

DOCTOR                        Not so sick my lord, *[annotation: with the old version of himself]*
          As she is troubled with thick-coming fancies *[annotation: delusions]*
          That keep her from her rest.

MACBETH *[annotation: talks about himself]* Cure her of that.
          *[annotation left: make her forget. losophical: you could, could you?]*
          Canst thou not minister to a mind diseased, *[annotation: nature of guilt. he needs oblivion. 40]*
          Pluck from the memory a rooted sorrow,
          Raze out the written troubles of the brain,
          And with some sweet oblivious antidote
          Cleanse the stuffed bosom of that perilous stuff
          Which weighs upon the heart?

DOCTOR                        Therein the patient    45
          Must minister to himself. *[annotation: knows he talks about himself]*

MACBETH   Throw physic to the dogs, I'll none of it.

Macbeth asks the doctor to treat his country as if it were a patient. He should analyse her urine, discover what the disease is and cure it by purging. He asks what would get rid of the English army. Having previously demanded to have his armour put on, he now tells the attendant to take it off.

| | |
|---|---|
| **48** | **staff** army commander's baton |
| **49** | **send out** A repetition of his order to send more horsemen. |
| **50** | **Come sir, dispatch** Come on, hurry |
| **50–1** | **cast The water** diagnose the disease by testing urine |
| **52** | **purge** cleanse, clear it out |
| | **pristine** former |
| **54** | **should applaud again** the echo would seem to redouble the applause |
| | **Pull 't off** Take off my armour |
| **55** | **rhubarb, senna** Plants known for their laxative properties. |
| **56** | **scour ... hence** remove these English |
| | **Hear'st ... them?** Have you heard about the English? |
| **58** | **Bring it after me** Follow me with the armour |
| **59** | **bane** destruction in whatever shape it might come: murder, death in battle, single combat |
| **62** | **Profit ... here** I would not come back here whatever I was paid |

Come, put mine armour on; give me my staff.
Seyton, send out. Doctor, the thanes fly from me.
[*To attendant*] Come sir, dispatch. If thou couldst,
    doctor, cast                                 50
The water of my land, find her disease,
And purge it to a sound and pristine health,
I would applaud thee to the very echo,
That should applaud again. [*To attendant*] Pull 't
    off I say.
[*To* DOCTOR] What rhubarb, senna, or what
    purgative drug, ) *Laxative?*               55
Would scour these English hence? Hear'st thou of
    them?

DOCTOR    Ay my good lord; your royal preparation
Makes us hear something.

MACBETH                  [*To attendant*] Bring it after me.
I will not be afraid of death and bane,
Till Birnam forest come to Dunsinane.      60

                     [*Exeunt all but* DOCTOR

DOCTOR    Were I from Dunsinane away, and clear,
Profit again should hardly draw me here.

*He's gone*

# Act 5 scenes 1 to 3

## The sleepwalking scene

You are going to prepare a performance of the central part of this scene. The actor playing the part of Lady Macbeth has to think about:

- what is going on in Lady Macbeth's head as she sleepwalks
- the pictures she sees and the sounds she imagines
- what she does as she speaks.

You can break her speeches down like this:

| Lines | Mental pictures | Actions |
|-------|-----------------|---------|
| Out damned spot, out I say! | On her hand, a spot of blood that she cannot get rid of. | She rubs her hands to remove the spot. |
| One, two; why then 'tis time to do 't | It is the night when they killed Duncan. She hears the clock chiming. Macbeth is with her. | She listens to the bell, then speaks to her imagined Macbeth. |
|  |  |  |

**Work in a group of three**

1 Read silently lines 35–67.

2 Each take one of these sections to work on:
- lines 35–40
- lines 42–5 and 49–51
- lines 60–67

3 Make a table like the one above for your chosen lines.

4 When you have all finished, pass around your tables and discuss them. Can any of you make other suggestions for each section?

5 Now discuss how you could perform lines 35–67.

6 Cast the parts and rehearse the scene.

# Staging scene 3

The last act of *Macbeth* is full of action; as things begin to close in on him, Macbeth's speech and actions become increasingly frantic.

### Work in a group of four

1   Imagine that you are directing a performance of the play in Shakespeare's Globe. If you need to refresh your memory look again at the description and pictures on pages xiv-xvii.

2   Discuss the whole scene. Decide what is outside each of the doors and what (if anything) is in the inner stage.

3   Each take one of these sections of the scene:

- lines 1–19
- lines 31–46
- lines 19–30
- lines 47–62

### Work on your own

4   Read your lines carefully to get a picture in your mind of where the characters are and what they do as the scene develops.

5   Pick two or three key moments in your section. Draw a plan to show where all the actors are at that moment, and write in their words, like this:

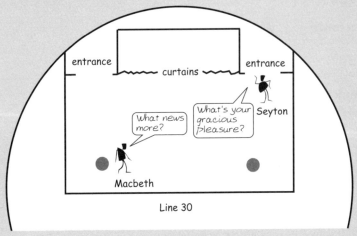

Line 30

### Rejoin your group

When you have all finished, share and discuss your ideas.

## Scene 2: the language of the text

This scene contains some startling images. In many of them, something that is abstract is described in a vividly physical way. For example:

*Revenges burn in them...* (line 3)
*Now does he feel | His secret murders sticking on his hands.*
(lines 16–17)
*Now does he feel his title | Hang loose about him, like a giant's robe | Upon a dwarfish thief.* (lines 20–2)

Here is the start of a mind map to explore the first of these images:

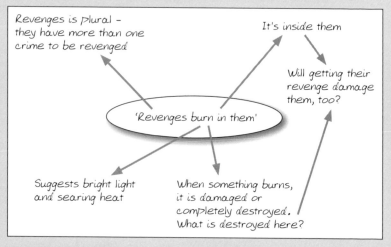

**Work with a partner**

1 Each take one of the other images. Take a large sheet of paper and use a mind map to explore your chosen image.

2 When you have both finished, swap papers. See if you can add other ideas to your partner's mind map.

3 Read through the whole scene and find two more vivid images.

4 Take one each and go through steps 1 and 2 again.

5 Discuss an answer to this question:

How do the images in this scene help us to understand the characters' thoughts and feelings?

# Plot summary quiz

The 12 short quotations below sum up the story of these scenes.

1  Work out the correct order for them.
2  Work out who said each one.

**A**

Canst thou not minister to a mind diseased,
Pluck from the memory a rooted sorrow…?

**B**

Foul whisperings are abroad. Unnatural deeds
Do breed unnatural troubles…

**C**

Great Dunsinane he strongly fortifies.
Some say he's mad…

**D**

I have lived long enough. My way of life
Is fallen into the sear, the yellow leaf…

**E**

Lo you, here she comes. This is her very guise, and upon my life, fast asleep.

**F**

Make we our march towards Birnam.

**G**

Till Birnam wood remove to Dunsinane,
I cannot taint with fear.

**H**

Were I from Dunsinane away, and clear,
Profit again should hardly draw me here.

**I**

What, will these hands ne'er be clean?

**J**

What's done cannot be undone. To bed, to bed, to bed.

**K**

When was it she last walked?

**L**

Yet who would have thought the old man to have had so much blood in him?

The English forces have met the Scots at Birnam Wood. Malcolm orders them all to carry a branch from the trees so that the enemy will not be able to see how many of them there are. They know that more of Macbeth's men have left him.

2      **chambers ... safe** men will be safe in their beds

         **We doubt it nothing** We have no doubt at all

5      **shadow** disguise

6      **host** army

6–7   **make discovery ... us** make any spies misjudge our numbers

8      **no other but** no other news than that

9–10  **endure ... before 't** not stop us laying siege to it

11     **advantage to be gone** opportunity to leave

12     **more ... revolt** nobles and commoners have deserted him

13     **constrained things** conscripted wretches

14–15 **Let our ... event** Let us see if our opinions are accurate when the battle takes place

15–16 **put we ... soldiership** let us take full military precautions

17     **due decision** the eventual outcome

18     **what we ... owe** what is our strength, and what we are lacking

19     **Thoughts ... relate** Guesses may express false hopes

## Scene 4

*Enter, with drum and colours,* MALCOLM, SIWARD *and*
YOUNG SIWARD, MACDUFF, MENTEITH, CAITHNESS, ANGUS,
LENNOX, ROSS, *and soldiers, marching*

MALCOLM   Cousins, I hope the days are near at hand
          That chambers will be safe.

MENTEITH                              We doubt it nothing.

SIWARD    What wood is this before us?   *For audience to*

MENTEITH                              The wood of Birnam.   *know.*

MALCOLM   Let every soldier hew him down a bough,
          And bear 't before him. Thereby shall we shadow      5
          The numbers of our host, and make discovery
          Err in report of us.

SOLDIERS                    It shall be done.

SIWARD    We learn no other but the confident tyrant
          Keeps still in Dunsinane, and will endure
          Our setting down before 't.

MALCOLM                       'Tis his main hope.      10

*They got the advantage*

          For where there is advantage to be gone,
          Both more and less have given him the revolt,
          And none serve with him but constrained things,
          Whose hearts are absent too.

MACDUFF                         Let our just censures
          Attend the true event, and put we on      15
          Industrious soldiership.

SIWARD                       The time approaches

*let's fight.*

          That will with due decision make us know
          What we shall say we have, and what we owe.
          Thoughts speculative their unsure hopes relate,

**20**     **But certain ... arbitrate** a definite result can only be decided by battle

Macbeth is confident that he can withstand a siege. Seyton brings him the news that Lady Macbeth is dead.

**1**       **Hang ... walls** This will show that Macbeth is in residence.

**4**       **ague** fever

**5**       **Were they ... ours** If they had not been reinforced with men who should have been on our side

**6**       **dareful ... beard** boldly, face to face

**10**      **The time has been** There was a time when

            **my senses ... cooled** I would have gone cold

**11**      **night-shriek** cry in the night

            **fell of hair** skin, scalp

**11–12**   **my fell ... stir** when I heard a horror story, my hair would stand on end

**13**      **As life were in't** as if it were alive

            **supped ... horrors** I have had my fill of horrors

**14–15**   **Direness ... me** horror, always a part of my murderous thoughts, can no longer upset me

**17**      **hereafter** later 1) after a normal life span 2) when I could deal with this news and mourn

**18**      **a time ... word** a proper time to die

But certain issue strokes must arbitrate;                    20
Towards which advance the war.

[*Exeunt, marching*

*war.*

## Scene 5

*Enter, with drum and colours,* MACBETH, SEYTON,
*and soldiers*

MACBETH     Hang out our banners on the outward walls.
            The cry is still, 'They come'. Our castle's strength

*safer in
the
castle.*

            Will laugh a siege to scorn. Here let them lie
            Till famine and the ague eat them up.

*'s own men*

            Were they not forced with those that should be
            ours,                                               5

*turnt
against him.*

            We might have met them dareful, beard to beard,
            And beat them backward home.

                                [*A cry of women within*
                        What is that noise?

SEYTON      It is the cry of women, my good lord. *servants.
                                          because L. MB
                                          [*Exit*  is ded*

MACBETH     I have almost forgot the taste of fears.
            The time has been, my senses would have cooled    10
            To hear a night-shriek, and my fell of hair
            Would at a dismal treatise rouse and stir     *associates
            As life were in't. I have supped full with horrors; *horrors to
            Direness, familiar to my slaughterous thoughts,  celebration*
            Cannot once start me. *FS → something will affect
                                                          him.*

*Enter* SEYTON

                        Wherefore was that cry?          15
SEYTON      The Queen, my lord, is dead. *plain he doesnt give
                                               a hoot.*
MACBETH     She should have died hereafter;
            There would have been a time for such a word.

*Death*          *It was more
            indirect for MD
            because          (191)
            ppl like him.*

Macbeth reflects on the insignificance of life. A messenger reports that Birnam Wood is moving towards Dunsinane. Macbeth decides that there is no point in waiting or in running away, and he goes to meet the enemy.

**19**      **Tomorrow ... tomorrow** A pointless succession of days

**20**      **Creeps ... to day** time is measured in this meaningless way

**21**      **To the ... time** until the record of our life ends on Judgement Day

**22**      **all our yesterdays** every day that we have lived through

**22–3**      **all our ... death** every day has shown fools the way to the grave

**23**      **brief candle** that short-lived light which is life

**24–6**      **Life's but ... more** Life is like a moving shadow, making no impression, or a bad actor who walks on stage and makes a great show of performing for a short time but is never heard of again

**27**      **sound and fury** words and emotion

**28**      **Signifying nothing** it is meaningless

**29**      **to use thy tongue** with a message for me

**34**      **anon methought** presently it seemed to me

**36**      **endure your wrath** put up with your anger

**40**      **famine cling thee** you shrivel from starvation

        **sooth** truth

**41**      **I care ... much** you are welcome to do the same for me

**42**      **I pull in resolution** I rein in my conviction (He is beginning to lose confidence.)

**43–4**      **th' equivocation ... truth** the double-talking of the devil when he means to deceive, so that lies sound like truth

**46**      **Arm ... out!** To arms, attack!

**47**      **If this... appear** If what he has declared does come true

**48**      **There ... here** there is no point either in fleeing or in waiting here

*Time means nothing anymore.*

(Tomorrow, and tomorrow, and tomorrow,)
Creeps in this petty pace from day to day,    20
To the last syllable of recorded time;
*Fools have* (And all our yesterdays have lighted fools
*died every* The way to dusty death) Out, out, brief (candle!) *Life*
*day .* (Life's but a walking shadow,) a poor player, *Life isn't real*
That struts and frets his hour upon the stage,    25
And then is heard no more (It is a tale
Told by an idiot, full of sound and fury,    *just actors.*
Signifying nothing.) *Catharsis - audience feels*

*Enter a* MESSENGER    *his pain .*

Thou comest to use thy tongue. Thy story quickly.

MESSENGER   Gracious my lord,      30
I should report that which I say I saw,
But know not how to do 't.

MACBETH         Well, say, sir.

MESSENGER   As I did stand my watch upon the hill,
I looked toward Birnam, and anon methought
The wood began to move.

MACBETH         Liar and slave! *scared* 35

MESSENGER   Let me endure your wrath, if 't be not so.
Within this three mile may you see it coming.
I say, a moving grove.

MACBETH         If thou speak'st false,
Upon the next tree shalt thou hang alive *Trees associated*
Till famine cling thee. If thy speech be sooth,   *to death*
I care not if thou dost for me as much.
I pull in resolution, and begin
To doubt th' equivocation of the fiend,
That lies like truth: 'Fear not, till Birnam wood
*now he* Do come to Dunsinane'; (and now a wood    45
*knows he'll* Comes toward Dunsinane.) Arm, arm, and out! *Fear drive*
*die* If this which he avouches does appear,   *him out*
There is nor flying hence, nor tarrying here. *of the*
                        *castle*
                       *where he*
                       *would've been*
                         *safe*

| | |
|---|---|
| **49** | **I 'gin ... sun** I am growing tired of daily life |
| **50** | **And wish ... undone** And wish the whole world could be destroyed |
| **51** | **wrack** ruin |
| **52** | **harness** armour |

The attacking army throw down their branches, and Malcolm gives the order to begin fighting.

| | |
|---|---|
| **2** | **uncle** i.e. Old Siward |
| **4** | **first battle** main army |
| **5** | **upon 's** upon us |
| **6** | **order** plan, arrangement |
| **7** | **Do we ... tonight** If we meet with the tyrant's army |
| **10** | **clamorous harbingers** noisy heralds |

Macbeth has no choice; he must fight.

| | |
|---|---|
| **1** | **tied ... stake** (like a bear about to be baited by dogs) |
| **2** | **fight the course** fight this engagement |
| | **What's he** What sort of man is he |

I 'gin to be aweary of the sun,
And wish th' estate o' th' world were now undone.  50
Ring the alarum bell! Blow wind, come wrack,
At least we'll die with harness on our back

*comforts him.*  *As a warrior.*

[*Exeunt*

## Scene 6

*Enter, with drum and colours,* MALCOLM, SIWARD,
MACDUFF, *etc., and their army, with boughs*

*misleading: use branches to seem greater in no.*

MALCOLM    Now near enough; your leafy screens throw down,
And show like those you are. You, worthy uncle,
Shall with my cousin your right noble son,
Lead our first battle. Worthy Macduff and we
Shall take upon 's what else remains to do.          5
According to our order.

SIWARD                              Fare you well.
Do we but find the tyrant's power tonight,
Let us be beaten, if we cannot fight.

MACDUFF    Make all our trumpets speak, give them all breath,
Those clamorous harbingers of blood and death.       10

[*Exeunt. Alarums*

## Scene 7

*Alarums. Enter* MACBETH

MACBETH    They have tied me to a stake. I cannot fly,
But bear-like I must fight the course. What's he
That was not born of woman? Such a one
Am I to fear, or none.

Macbeth kills Young Siward, but Macduff is getting close to him. Old Siward tells Malcolm that the castle has been taken.

**10**   **abhorred** hateful, offensive

**13**   **Brandished** wielded

**15**   **If thou ... mine** If you are killed without my having struck the blow

**16**   **still** for ever

**17**   **kerns** Irish mercenaries

**18**   **staves** clubs

**20**   **undeeded** unused

**21–2** **By this ... bruited** This great noise would seem to suggest someone of great importance

**24**   **the castle's gently rendered** the castle has been surrendered without a fight

**27**   **The day ... yours** you have almost won the day

*Enter* YOUNG SIWARD

YOUNG SIWARD  What is thy name?  *The devil*

MACBETH                                          (Thou'lt be afraid to hear it.)     5

YOUNG SIWARD  No, though thou call'st thyself a hotter name
              Than any is in hell. *worse than the Devil.*

MACBETH                              My name's Macbeth.

YOUNG SIWARD  The devil himself could not pronounce a title
              More hateful to mine ear.                     *Accepts*

MACBETH                              No, nor more fearful.   *it.*

YOUNG SIWARD  Thou liest, abhorred tyrant. With my sword      10
              I'll prove the lie thou speak'st.
                                                            *young &*
                    [*They fight, and* YOUNG SIWARD *is slain* ] *honourable*

MACBETH                    Thou wast born of woman.   *die*
              But swords I smile at, weapons laugh to scorn,
              Brandished by man that's of a woman born. *muahhaha*
                                                        [*Exit*

*evil* /

*Alarums. Enter* MACDUFF

MACDUFF        That way the noise is. Tyrant, show thy face.
*warns revenge* If thou be'st slain, and with no stroke of mine,     15
*supernatural*  My wife and children's ghosts will haunt me still. *feels*
               I cannot strike at wretched kerns, whose arms  *guilt*
               Are hired to bear their staves. Either thou,
                   Macbeth, *#1* *MB can't do it himself*
               Or else my sword, with an unbattered edge
               I sheath again undeeded. There thou shouldst
                   be;                                         20
               By this great clatter, one of greatest note
               Seems bruited. Let me find him, fortune,
               And more I beg not.
                                              [*Exit. Alarums*

*Enter* MALCOLM *and* SIWARD

SIWARD         This way my lord, the castle's gently rendered.
               The tyrant's people on both sides do fight. *some of them*
               The noble thanes do bravely in the war;        *have turnt*
               The day almost itself professes yours,          *sides.*

197

**28–9** **We ... beside us** We have recognised enemies who have fought side by side with us

Macduff finds Macbeth. They begin to fight, but Macbeth tells Macduff that he is wasting his time because no man born of woman can hurt him. Macduff says that he was born by Caesarean operation.

**1** **the Roman fool** The honourable end for the defeated Roman soldier was to commit suicide by falling on his sword. In this way he avoided being part of his enemy's triumph.

**2–3** **Whiles ... upon them** As long as I can see live enemies, it is better to see the gashes on them

**4** **Of all men else** More than all other men

**5** **charged** burdened

**8** **terms ... out** any words can describe

**Thou losest labour** You are wasting your effort

**9** **the intrenchant** that cannot be cut, cannot be hurt

**9–10** **may'st ... me bleed** it would be as much use slashing away at the air with your sharp sword as trying to make me bleed

**11** **vulnerable crests** heads that can be wounded

**12** **must not yield** cannot give way

**13** **Despair thy charm** Lose all trust in your charm

**14** **angel ... served** evil angel you have always served

**16** **Untimely** before time, prematurely (Macduff was delivered by Caesarean section, and could therefore be said not to have been 'born'.)

And little is to do.

MALCOLM                              We have met with foes
That strike beside us.

SIWARD                                          Enter, sir, the castle.

[*Exeunt. Alarum*

## Scene 8

*Enter* MACBETH

MACBETH    (Why should I play the Roman fool, and die
*Suicide is*    On mine own sword?)Whiles I see lives, the gashes
*not an*        Do better upon them.  *wants to kill*
*option for*
*him*           *Enter* MACDUFF

MACDUFF                           Turn, hell-hound, turn!    *Macduff*
MACBETH    (Of all men else I have avoided thee.)  *"Beware Had"*
But get thee back, my soul is too much charged        5
With blood of thine already.           *1st. apparition*

MACDUFF                              I have no words:
My voice is in my sword, thou bloodier villain
Than terms can give thee out!

[*They fight*

MACBETH                            Thou losest labour;
As easy may'st thou the intrenchant air
With thy keen sword impress, as make me bleed.    10
Let fall thy blade on vulnerable crests;
(I bear a charmed life, which must not yield
To one of woman born.)  *convinces himself that*
                        *he's not a threat.*
MACDUFF                        Despair thy charm,
And let the angel whom thou still hast served )*Lucifer.*
Tell thee Macduff was from his mother's womb        15
Untimely ripped.      *Oh Shit*

199

Macbeth realises he has been deceived. He is completely unmanned and refuses to fight on. Macduff says Macbeth will be taken around the countryside like a fairground freak. At this threat Macbeth fights and is killed.

| | |
|---|---|
| **18** | **cowed ... man** intimidated my manly spirit, made me a coward |
| **19** | **juggling** cheating, using words with double meanings |
| **20** | **palter ... sense** trick us with double meanings |
| **21–2** | **keep ... hope** keep that promise whispered in our ears but break that promise when we hope it will come true |
| **24** | **show ... time** spectacle of our age (Macbeth will be paraded through the streets and laughed at.) |
| **25** | **rarer monsters** more special freaks |
| **26** | **Painted ... underwrit** advertised by a painting on a sign, with this caption |
| **28** | **kiss the ground** The image is strong, the meaning 'humble myself'. |
| **29** | **rabble** commoners |
| **31** | **thou opposed** you, my opponent |
| **32** | **I will ... last** I will do all that is left to me, to fight to the end |
| **33** | **Lay on** Fight on |

The victorious army is counting its losses.

| | |
|---|---|
| **1** | **we miss** who are missing |
| **2** | **go off** die |
| | **by these** judging by these already here |

MACBETH    Accursed be that tongue that tells me so,
           For it hath cowed my better part of man. *) scared.*
           And be these juggling fiends no more believed,
           That palter with us in a double sense, *) equivocation.*
           That keep the word of promise to our ear,
           And break it to our hope. I'll not fight with thee.

MACDUFF    Then yield thee, coward,
           And live to be the show and gaze o' th' time.
           We'll have thee, as our rarer monsters are,          25
           Painted upon a pole, and underwrit,          *Refered as a*
           'Here may you see the tyrant.'          *monster- humiliate*

MACBETH                    (I will not yield,)  *Fights*
*True*     To kiss the ground before young Malcolm's feet,  *untill the*
*lineage*  And to be baited with the rabble's curse.          *end.*
           Though Birnam wood be come to Dunsinane,
           And thou opposed, being of no woman born,
           Yet I will try the last. Before my body
*Last*     I throw my warlike shield. Lay on Macduff,
*words.*   And damned be him that first cries 'Hold, enough!'

                              [Exeunt, fighting. Alarums
           *They enter fighting and* MACBETH *is slain*   *Action,*
                                                           *big*
                                                           *fight.*

## Scene ❾

           *Retreat. Flourish. Enter, with drum and colours,*
           MALCOLM, SIWARD, ROSS, LENNOX, ANGUS, CAITHNESS,
           MENTEITH, *and soldiers*

MALCOLM    I would the friends we miss were safe arrived.

SIWARD     Some must go off; and yet by these I see,
           So great a day as this is cheaply bought.

MALCOLM    Macduff is missing, and your noble son.

Siward learns of his son's death, and refuses to mourn for him because he did his duty and so is in God's care. Macduff brings in Macbeth's head on a stake. Malcolm promises to reward all those who deserve it.

| | |
|---|---|
| **5** | **paid a soldier's debt** been killed |
| **6–7** | **till ... confirmed** no sooner did his bravery confirm he was a man |
| **7** | **prowess** bravery |
| **8** | **In the ... fought** in the post where he fought without flinching |
| **9** | **But ... died** then he died like a man |
| **12** | **before** in front (He was facing the enemy, not running away.) |
| **13** | **on the front** on the forehead, on the face |
| **14** | **as I have hairs** (on my head) A **pun** on 'heirs' (see Glossary p. 242). |
| **16** | **knell is knolled** death bell has been rung (and there is no more to be said) |
| **18** | **parted ... score** died bravely and did his duty |
| **19** | **newer comfort** more good news |
| **21** | **The time is free** This age has recovered its freedom |
| **22** | **compassed ... pearl** surrounded by 1) your most loyal thanes 2) the jewelled crown of Scotland |
| **23** | **salutation** greeting, their declaration of homage to you |
| **26** | **We shall ... time** We shall not be long |
| **27** | **reckon ... loves** reward the loyalty of each of you |
| **28** | **make ... you** pay our debts to you |

ROSS  Your son, my lord, has paid a soldier's debt. *heroically* *not like MB* 5
He only lived but till he was a man,
The which no sooner had his prowess confirmed
In the unshrinking station where he fought,
But like a man he died.

SIWARD                      Then he is dead?

ROSS  Ay, and brought off the field. Your cause of sorrow 10
Must not be measured by his worth, for then
It hath no end.

SIWARD                      Had he his hurts before?

ROSS  Ay, on the front.

SIWARD                      Why then, God's soldier be he.
Had I as many sons as I have hairs,
I would not wish them to a fairer death. 15
And so, his knell is knolled.

MALCOLM                      He's worth more sorrow,
And that I'll spend for him. *Sorrow later.*

SIWARD                      He's worth no more.
They say he parted well, and paid his score.
And so God be with him. Here comes newer comfort.

*Re-enter* MACDUFF, *with* MACBETH's *head*

MACDUFF  Hail, King, for so thou art. Behold where stands 20
Th' usurper's cursed head. The time is free. *Best of all*
I see thee compassed with thy kingdom's pearl, *Scotland*
That speak my salutation in their minds;
Whose voices I desire aloud with mine:
Hail, King of Scotland!

*Happy ending*

ALL                      Hail, King of Scotland! 25

*Hail Malcolm.*

MALCOLM  We shall not spend a large expense of time
Before we reckon with your several loves,
And make us even with you. My thanes and
        kinsmen,  *Thank for loyalty*

Malcolm intends to hunt down all those who committed atrocities for Macbeth. He says it is thought that Lady Macbeth committed suicide. He invites all those present to his coronation.

**30**      **In such ... named** named with this honourable title

**31**      **planted ... time** established at the beginning of this new age

**33**      **snares ... tyranny** Traps where spies posted by the tyrant were always watching.

**34–5**      **Producing ... queen** seeking out those evil men who acted for this wicked butcher and the monster who was his queen

**36–7**      **by self ... life** committed suicide

**38**      **Grace** God

**39**      **in measure** appropriately, in due proportion

**40**      **all at once** all of you together

        **to each one** to each of you individually

no more thanes.

Henceforth be (earls,) the first that ever Scotland

everything
is
changing

In such an honour named. What's more to do,          30
Which would be planted newly with the time –
As calling home our exiled friends abroad,     HB is
That fled the snares of watchful tyranny,       barren.
Producing forth the cruel ministers
Of this dead butcher and his fiend-like queen,   35   4th witch.
Who as 'tis thought, by self and violent hands
Took off her life – this, and what needful else    suicide.
That calls upon us, by the grace of Grace,
We will perform in measure, time and place.
So thanks to all at once, and to each one,          40
Whom we invite to see us crowned at Scone.

From warrior to butcher.   [*Flourish. Exeunt*

# Act 5 scenes 4 to 9

## Battle scenes

In this part of the play, Shakespeare shows us a large army moving towards Macbeth's castle of Dunsinane and then the battle in which many soldiers, including Macbeth, were killed. All this has to be done in a limited space and with a small number of actors. Shakespeare overcomes these difficulties by giving us a number of short scenes in which the action moves rapidly from place to place.

**Work on your own**

1   Look through scenes 4 to 9 and then copy and complete the table below. It has been started for you.

| Scene | Number of speaking characters | Where it takes place | Main actions |
|-------|-------------------------------|----------------------|--------------|
| 4 | 4 | Birnam Wood | The rebel army is on the march. |
| 5 | 3 | | |
| 6 | | | |
| 7 | | | |
| 8 | | | |
| 9 | | | |

**Work in a group of four**

2   You are going to plan a touring production of the play.

   **a**   You only have ten actors in your company, so each will have to play more than one part, using small changes of costume to show who they are. Some non-speaking characters will have to be cut.

   **b**   You will be playing in different spaces: school halls, leisure centres, and village halls. Some will be small with few facilities.

   Discuss how these battle scenes can be made as dramatic as possible.

3   Choose two from scenes 4, 6, 7, and 8.

4   Make a set of notes explaining how you will produce these scenes.

# Drama: thought-tracking scene 5

A character's speeches in a play are only the outward sign of what that person is actually thinking. Sometimes they may deliberately conceal their true thoughts. We can explore the relationship between what they say and what they think by thought-tracking.

**Work in a group of six**

1   Read silently lines 1–15.

2   Cast the parts like this:

   • Macbeth's words
   • Macbeth's thoughts
   • Seyton's words
   • Seyton's thoughts

3   Now act the lines like this:

   a   The 'words' actors perform the lines.

   b   The 'thoughts' actors move with them. At key moments, a 'thoughts' actor says 'Freeze!'

   c   Then that 'thoughts' actor speaks the character's thoughts at that point.

   d   The other 'thoughts' actor can follow this with their thoughts, if they wish.

4   Before you begin, allow a moment for the 'thoughts' actors to think about when they will pause the action and what they will say. Then begin the scene.

5   Now change the casting round, and add the Messenger's words and the Messenger's thoughts.

6   Perform the rest of the scene in a similar way.

# Macbeth's despair

In scene 5 Macbeth learns of his wife's death. In a short speech, of only 12 lines, he expresses his response to the news.

**Work with a partner**

1 Copy the table below.

2 Use the spaces to explain what you think each expression tells us about Macbeth's thoughts and feelings. One has been done for you.

| Line(s) | What he says | What it tells us |
|---------|--------------|------------------|
| 17–18 | She should have died ... such a word. | He can't handle this at the moment with everything else going on: he needs more time. |
| 19–21 | Tomorrow ... recorded time. | |
| 22–3 | And all our yesterdays ... dusty death. | |
| 23 | Out, out, brief candle! | |
| 24–6 | Life's but a walking shadow ... heard no more. | |
| 26–8 | It is a tale ... Signifying nothing. | |

**Work in a group of four**

3 Swap your filled-out tables and share your ideas.

4 You are going to prepare a group reading of this speech. Break the speech into sections. You can use the sections in the table, or make your own.

5 Each section can be spoken by one person, or two or more speaking together. Decide who will speak which section(s).

6 Think about speed and volume. Plan where you will have pauses.

7 Now practise your reading.

# Quotation quiz

For each of these quotations, work out:

1 who said it

2 who they were speaking to

3 what it tells us about

   **a** the speaker

   **b** the situation

   **c** any other characters.

**A**
> But swords I smile at, weapons laugh to scorn,
> Brandished by man that's of a woman born.

**B**
> Had I as many sons as I have hairs,
> I would not wish them to a fairer death.

**C**
> Hail, King, for so thou art.
> Behold where stands
> Th' usurper's cursed head.
> The time is free.

**D**
> I looked toward Birnam, and anon methought
> The wood began to move.

**E**
> It is a tale
> Told by an idiot, full of sound and fury,
> Signifying nothing.

**F**
> My voice is in my sword…

**G**
> Our castle's strength
> Will laugh a siege to scorn.

**H**
> She should have died hereafter;
> There would have been a time for such a word.

**I**
> The devil himself could not pronounce a title
> More hateful to mine ear…

**J**
> They have tied me to a stake; I cannot fly,
> But bear-like I must fight the course.

| Act 1 |
| --- |
| Macbeth has won two great victories. The witches prophesy that he will be king, and that Banquo will be the ancestor of kings. When King Duncan names Malcolm as his successor, Macbeth begins to contemplate murder. Lady Macbeth, inspired by Macbeth's letter, is determined to help him become king. Duncan stays with them overnight, and she persuades Macbeth to go ahead with plans for Duncan's murder. |
| **Act 2** |
| Macbeth kills Duncan and is shaken by what he has done. The guards are suspected of being involved, but Macbeth has killed them too. Duncan's sons, Malcolm and Donalbain, fear for their lives and flee. |
| **Act 3** |
| Aware of the witches' prophecy to Banquo, Macbeth hires two murderers. They kill Banquo, but Fleance escapes. Banquo's ghost appears to Macbeth at the banquet, and Macbeth is paralysed with horror. Lady Macbeth asks the guests to leave. Macbeth is angry that Macduff is avoiding him. He decides to visit the witches again to find out what the future holds. |
| **Act 4** |
| The apparitions seem to give Macbeth comforting news but the show of kings upsets him. Macbeth orders the death of Macduff's family. Malcolm prepares an army to oppose Macbeth. |
| **Act 5** |
| Lady Macbeth breaks down under the strain of recent events. Macbeth, deserted by most of his followers, is also becoming frenzied. Malcolm and the English army are reinforced by many Scots who want to see the end of Macbeth. Lady Macbeth dies. The battle of Dunsinane is quickly over. Macbeth is killed by Macduff and Malcolm is proclaimed king. |

| Act/Scene | Action | Theme/Summary |
|---|---|---|
| 1.1 | The three witches | Influence of supernatural |
| 1.2 | The captain's report | Macbeth's reputation |
| 1.3 | The prophecies | Macbeth's ambition stirred |
| 1.4 | Duncan's gratitude | Malcolm heir to throne |
| 1.5 | Macbeth's letter | Lady Macbeth's reaction |
| 1.6 | Duncan visits Macbeth | The saintly king |
| 2.1 | 'Is this a dagger...?' | Macbeth troubled |
| 2.2 | Duncan's murder | Macbeth's conscience |
| 2.3 | Body discovered | The Macbeths are defensive |
| 2.4 | Ross and the old man | Natural world in disorder |
| 3.1 | Murderers hired | Attempt to defy prophecy |
| 3.2 | Lady Macbeth not told | Macbeth continues evil course |
| 3.3 | Banquo's murder | Escape of Fleance |
| 3.4 | Banquo's ghost | Strain is showing |
| 3.5 | Hecate and the witches | Reinforcement of supernatural |
| 3.6 | Lennox and a lord | Suspicions about Macbeth |
| 4.1 | The apparitions | Macbeth given encouragement |
| 4.2 | Macduff's wife and children killed | Height of Macbeth's evil |
| 4.3 | Macduff sees Malcolm | Macbeth's opponents organised |
| 5.1 | Sleepwalking scene | Lady Macbeth's deterioration |
| 5.2 | Scottish soldiers | Opposition to Macbeth grows |
| 5.3 | Macbeth at Dunsinane | Macbeth confident but frantic |
| 5.4 | Malcolm at Birnam Wood | The 3rd apparition's warning is explained |
| 5.5 | Lady Macbeth's death | 'Moving wood' daunts Macbeth |
| 5.6 | Malcolm ready to fight | Macbeth almost alone |
| 5.7 | Death of Young Siward | Macduff stalks Macbeth |
| 5.8 | Death of Macbeth | 2nd apparition's prophecy is explained |
| 5.9 | Malcolm declared King | 1st apparition's prophecy is fulfilled |

In this section of the book there are activities and advice to help you explore the play in more detail:

On pages 238–44 there is a Glossary, which explains some of the technical terms that are used in the book.

# Character

## Macbeth and Lady Macbeth in Acts 1 and 2

When the lives of two or more people are closely connected, we often talk about their 'relationship'. Relationships can be based on a number of quite different things, including:

| | | |
|---|---|---|
| trust | shared interest | obedience |
| love | domination | loyalty |
| control | family ties | attraction |

**Work on your own**

1  Think about the relationship between the Macbeths.  Which of the above nine things apply to their relationship? Write them down.

2  Are there any other things that their relationship is based on? Add these to your list.

3  Now reduce your list to the five most important things that the Macbeths' relationship is based on. Use a table like the one below to explain each of your five choices and to provide some evidence to support each one.

| Chosen point | Reason for my choice | Evidence to support my choice |
|---|---|---|
| 1 | | |
| 2 | | |

## *Other relationships in the play*

There are many different relationships in Macbeth. These include:

- King/subject
- friends
- master/servant
- comrades-in-arms

**Work with a partner**

1  Make a list of examples of four different types of relationship in the play (other than the Macbeths' marriage).

2  Look at the four relationships you have listed. Explain what each relationship is based on, e.g. love, loyalty, obedience, power. Refer to evidence to support your ideas.

# Character X-ray

The Macbeths hide their true thoughts and feelings. Deception is an essential part of their strategy. As Lady Macbeth advises her husband,

> *...mock the time with fairest show:*
> *False face must hide what the false heart doth know.*
> (Act 1 scene 7 lines 81–2)

Because other characters begin to distrust Macbeth they too become guarded about their own true thoughts. To see into their minds we have to do a sort of character X-ray.

## *How to make a character X-ray:*

1  Choose one important moment in the play.

2  Around the edge of a large sheet of paper write the names of the characters who are on stage.

3  From each character draw an arrow to the character(s) who they are thinking about.

4  For each character draw a speech balloon. Inside it write a short summary of what they are saying

5  Give each character a thought bubble. In it write their real thoughts and feelings.

On the next page there is an example from Act 3 scene 4 lines 109–21.

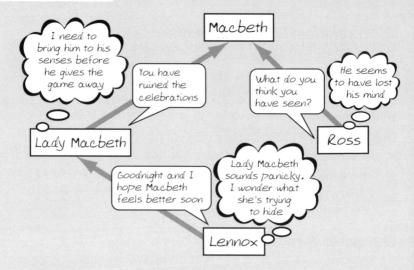

## *Make your own character X-rays*

6   Choose another important point in the play and do a character X-ray for it. You can choose your own, or take one from this list:

   • Act 1 scene 3 lines 100–17
   • Act 2 scene 3 lines 103–25
   • Act 5 scene 3 lines 37–54

# Character interpretation

Actors have to decide how their character is thinking and feeling in order to interpret that character and decide how to play them. They work closely with the director to develop an interpretation. During the performance each member of the audience then interprets the characters in their own way.

All of this means that in different productions of *Macbeth* characters can be presented in different ways. This is particularly true of the two central characters, Macbeth and Lady Macbeth. How the actors interpret these two characters depends on their answers to some key questions, such as:

•   Would Macbeth have killed Duncan if his wife had not persuaded him?

- When does he first consider killing Duncan?
- Who finally turns out to be more ruthless – Macbeth or Lady Macbeth?
- What finally makes Macbeth decide to kill Duncan? What does this suggest about him?
- Does Macbeth's attitude to his wife change as the play goes on?

**Work on your own**

1  Write down your answers to the questions above. Find evidence to support each of your answers.

**Work with a partner**

2  The best way to explore characters is to try acting them in different ways. For example, here are two different sets of performance guidelines for Act 3 scene 2 lines 4–56:

|  | Lady Macbeth | Macbeth |
|---|---|---|
| **Version one** | You are impatient with Macbeth and you are determined to control him. You wish he would be more 'manly'. | You are very nervous and under-confident. You regret what you have done. You would like to share your plans with your wife but you are afraid she would disapprove. |
| **Version two** | You are very worried about Macbeth and his state of mind. You regret what you have done: you know it was wrong and you know you won't get away with it. | You are patronising towards Lady Macbeth, but often you seem to be hardly aware of her presence. You are absorbed in your secret plans. You are full of confidence. |

Try out both versions described above to develop performances of these lines.

3  Choose another short section of the play. For example, you could use one of these sections:

- Act 2 scene 1 lines 10–30
- Act 5 scene 5 lines 7–38

4  Agree on brief performance guidelines for each character.

5  Perform the section with each of you sticking to the performance guidelines for your character.

6  Now agree new performance guidelines and act out the section again.

7  Discuss:

  a  Which set of guidelines worked better?

  b  Why?

  c  What other guidelines could you have used?

## Character development graph

Many characters change during the play. This is clearly true of the Macbeths and their relationship. The things they experience would change anyone.

A character development graph is a useful way of keeping track of changes in :

- a character
- the relationship between characters
- the way the audience feels about a character.

Here is an unfinished example:

**To what extent is Macbeth the dominant partner in his marriage?**

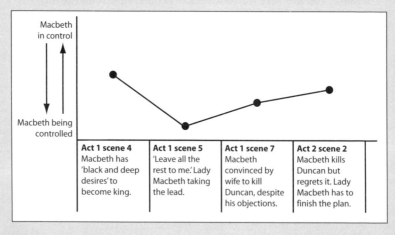

| Act 1 scene 4 | Act 1 scene 5 | Act 1 scene 7 | Act 2 scene 2 |
|---|---|---|---|
| Macbeth has 'black and deep desires' to become king. | 'Leave all the rest to me.' Lady Macbeth taking the lead. | Macbeth convinced by wife to kill Duncan, despite his objections. | Macbeth kills Duncan but regrets it. Lady Macbeth has to finish the plan. |

## Work in a small group

1   Copy the graph and extend it to the right to explore how the balance of power between the Macbeths develops during the rest of the play.

2   Make character development graphs of your own. Here are some topics worth charting in detail:

   **a**   Changes in Macbeth's levels of self-confidence.

   **b**   How other characters' trust and loyalty to Macbeth change.

   **c**   Changes in the audience's feelings towards Lady Macbeth.

**Important reminder:** When you create a development graph you are working with your own interpretation, and other interpretations are possible. That is why it is better to do this exercise with others who are willing to challenge your interpretations and force you to find evidence to support them.

# Drama and performance

## Thought-tracking

Thought-tracking is a way of exploring characters' thoughts and considering what 'makes them tick'. This is how to do it:

1   Choose a short and important section of the play.

2   Cast the parts, but give each character two actors. One actor should play the character; the other should play the character's thoughts and feelings.

3   Each 'thought' should stand by the shoulder of their character. The actors play the scene, but every so often a thought or a member of the audience says 'freeze'.

4   Then the actors stand still while the thoughts speak. It is often a good idea to speak the thoughts of the character who has been listening, as well as the one who has been speaking.

Try out thought-tracking for the following parts of the play:

• Act 2 scene 1 lines 10–30
• Act 2 scene 4 lines 21–40
• Act 4 scene 1 lines 135–43

## Hot-seating

Hot-seating is another way of 'getting inside' a character. It is a good preparation for acting. This is how it works:

1   One member of the class is given a character in a particular scene.

2   The character sits in the 'hot seat' with the class sitting around them in a semi-circle.

3   Class members take it in turns to ask the character in the hot seat questions about how they are feeling, why they said or did certain things, and so on.

4   The pupil in the hot seat has to answer these questions in role and without too much delay. (Their answers can be imaginative but they must make sense in terms of what we know from the play.)

## Example: Act 3 scene 6

Here are some questions Lennox might be asked in the hot seat:

- What did you say to the Lord before the scene started?
- How do you feel about Macbeth?
- Who do you think should go to England to get help?

# Tableau (or 'freeze-frame')

A tableau is like a film with the pause button pressed, so the actors freeze into position at a particular moment. Here's how to do it:

1  One member of your group is the director and helps you all to achieve the agreed expressions and postures.

2  Act out a scene and 'freeze' at different points. Your audience can comment on what each tableau suggests. Photograph the tableau to support further discussion.

You can prepare freeze-frames for other groups to see and comment on. Their first task is to work out which moment in the play has been frozen.

A tableau can be used in a more abstract way, to express a mood or idea. For example you might want to express 'victory' in Act 1 scene 2, or Macbeth's mood when he hears of his wife's death and delivers his 'She should have died hereafter' speech (Act 5 scene 5 lines 17–28).

## Darkness and death

The play is full of images, particularly images of darkness and death. For example:

- Act 2 scene 4 lines 7–10
- Act 3 scene 2 lines 51–4

Freeze-frames can be a powerful way of capturing and exploring these images.

### Work in a group of two to four

1  Create freeze-frames for the above two images.

2  Find two other examples of dark and/or light imagery. Create freeze-frames for those images.

# Statues and sculptures

Rulers often commission statues to mark great events or to celebrate important individuals. Getting together to 'sculpt' an actor (or actors) into a statue pose is another good opportunity to discuss the mood of a particular point in the play.

**Work in a group of three to five**

1   Imagine that at the end of Act 1 scene 4 Duncan has commissioned a statue of Macbeth and Banquo. Work together to sculpt a statue. Decide what feelings and ideas you want this statue to convey.

2   Now choose another statue from this list:

   a   Duncan (commissioned by Macbeth), Act 3 scene 1

   b   Lady Macduff (commissioned by Malcolm), Act 4 scene 3

   c   Lady Macbeth (commissioned by Macbeth), Act 5 scene 5

   d   Macbeth (commissioned by Malcolm), Act 5 scene 9

3   Again, work together to sculpt the statue. Decide what feelings and ideas you want this statue to convey.

4   Look at other groups' statues. Decide who they are statues of, and at what point in the play.

# Stepping out of the text

This is another way of exploring characters and 'bringing them to life', this time by wondering what those characters would be like in other situations – even impossible ones.

Some examples of out-of-text situations that you could use:

1   Imagine an assembly in your school with Macbeth as a visiting speaker. What does he say?

2   Imagine that Scotland is a sort of reality game show. The play's characters are evicted (banished) from Scotland one by one. Who goes? You decide. Interview each character on their eviction night.

3   What is life in Scotland like two years after the end of the play? Work on a scene involving some of the characters.

**Remember:** In out-of-text activities you must be able to justify what the characters say and do from what we know of them from the play. In other words, they must stay in role.

# Decision alley

Decision alley is a way of exploring some of the options that are open to characters (and the playwright) at certain points in the play. Here is how a decision alley works:

1 One person is a key character from the play.

2 The rest of the class stands in two lines facing each other down the length of the room, creating an 'alley'.

3 Each person in the alley thinks of some brief advice they would like to give the character about what s/he should do at this point in the play.

4 The character walks slowly down the alley, pausing by each person in the alley to hear their advice.

5 When the person playing the character reaches the end of the alley they should think aloud about the advice they have been given and explain what they have decided to do now.

Decision alley works best for moments in the play when a character is wrestling with their conscience to make a decision.

## *Sample situations*

Use an alley for one or more of the following situations:

**Act 1 scene 7**: To help Macbeth decide whether to kill Duncan. Each person in the alley could be one of the 'spirits' Lady Macbeth has called on to help her persuade Macbeth.

**Act 3 scene 1**: To help Banquo decide what to do in the light of his suspicions of Macbeth.

**Act 5 scene 1**: To help the Doctor decide what to do.

# Themes and issues

## Trust and betrayal

Disloyalty and betrayal govern Macbeth's behaviour increasingly as the play develops. Lady Macbeth's strategy from the outset is based on gaining people's trust in order to do away with them more effectively: 'look like th' innocent flower, I But be the serpent under't', she advises her husband (Act 1 scene 5 lines 65–6). Their home has an atmosphere that lulls visitors into a false sense of security. Duncan's first and fatal impression is that

> *This castle hath a pleasant seat. The air*
> *Nimbly and sweetly recommends itself*
> *Unto our gentle senses.*
> (Act 1 scene 6 lines 1–3)

Of course Duncan should have learned the lessons of trusting too easily: the Thane of Cawdor's treachery had almost led to Scotland's defeat in battle. 'He was a gentleman on whom I built I An absolute trust', Duncan declared on his execution.

Perhaps Macbeth's most shocking act of treachery is the murder of his closest friend, Banquo. To prepare the murder Macbeth carefully builds Banquo's trust to put him off guard: he says he looks forward to Banquo's company at that night's celebrations and flatters him as 'our chief guest' (Act 3 scene 1 line 11).

**Work on your own**

1 Read again the following scenes:

   **a** Act 1 scene 2

   **b** Act 1 scene 4

   **c** Act 1 scene 6

2 Make a list of the evidence they contain to suggest that Duncan is naturally a very trusting person.

3 Look carefully at the advice Lady Macbeth gives her husband in Act 1 scene 5 lines 62–72 ('Your face...' to '...is to fear').

4   Explain Lady Macbeth's advice.

5   Explain how she and Macbeth use this advice later in the play to carry out their plans.

# Ambition: personal or social?

Ambition is about what we want to achieve in the future. People often say it is good to have ambition because it gives us goals to strive for. People can have a wide range of ambitions. Some of these might be personal, such as to have a happy marriage or to become a doctor. Other ambitions might be more social than personal: for example, to do something effective about climate change or to serve your country. That sort of ambition would be likely to benefit many people.

Certainly Macbeth's sense of ambition is very strong. His description of it as 'vaulting' (Act 1 scene 7 line 27) suggests that it is hard to control, and Lady Macbeth has already acknowledged that her husband is 'not without ambition' (Act 1 scene 5 line 19).

**Work with a partner**

1   Find the moment when Macbeth first thinks of murdering Duncan. Find evidence to support your view.

2   To what extent is Macbeth's ambition to become king

   **a**   a personal one?

   **b**   based on a desire to serve his country?

   Try to provide evidence to support both sorts of ambition. (You might find more evidence for one than the other.)

3   Macbeth says he is driven by 'Vaulting ambition, which o'erleaps itself, | And falls on th' other' (Act 1 scene 7 lines 27–8).

   **a**   Look carefully at these words and the speech they complete.

   **b**   Explain what Macbeth means.

   **c**   Explain what these words might suggest about Macbeth's state of mind at this point in the play.

# Evil

The whole play is wrapped in a mood of evil and impending doom. This mood is helped by three major factors:

- The fact that the play's opening is dominated by the witches who revel in 'fog and filthy air' (Act 1 scene 1 line 12) and in the misfortunes they have inflicted on various people including a sailor and his wife (see Act 1 scene 3).
- The murky darkness and foul weather that dominate every scene. 'Darkness does the face of earth entomb', Ross observes after Duncan's murder (Act 2 scene 4 line 9).
- Macbeth's relentless violence, cruelty and cunning.

**Work on your own**

1 For each of the three points above choose one short section of the play in which the mood of evil is particularly strong.

2 For each of your choices explain:

a what the audience might think and feel at this point in the play

b how Shakespeare's choice of words emphasises the mood of evil.

You could choose your own sections or use these three:

- Witches: Act 4 scene 1 lines 1–48
- Darkness: Act 3 scene 2 lines 40–56
- Macbeth: Act 4 scene 1 lines 143–55

# Right and wrong

Despite their acts of cruelty both Macbeth and Lady Macbeth have to wrestle with their consciences. It is clear that they know the difference between right and wrong.

Although Lady Macbeth is willing to do anything to become queen, she has to call upon spirits to 'fill me from the crown to the toe top-full | Of direst cruelty' so that she will not be inhibited by her sense of 'remorse' (Act 1 scene 5 lines 42–3). Early in the play Macbeth battles with his conscience, constantly wavering in his decision to murder Duncan – an act that he recognises as 'deep damnation' (Act 1 scene

7 line 20). In other words it would be an offence not just against the king, but also against God.

**Work on your own**

1   Reread carefully the following lines:

   **a**   Act 1 scene 4 lines 50–2 ('Stars hide ... the hand')

   **b**   Act 1 scene 7 lines 12–25 ('He's here ... the wind')

   **c**   Act 2 scene 2 lines 71–2 ('To know ... thou couldst').

2   For each group of lines, explain the effect Macbeth's conscience has on the way he thinks, feels or behaves. Support your ideas by referring to details in the text. Explore your thinking by using a table like the one below:

| Lines | What this shows about Macbeth's conscience | Effects on how Macbeth thinks, behaves or feels | Evidence to support your ideas |
|---|---|---|---|
| Act 1 scene 4 lines 50–2 ('Stars hide ... the hand') | | | |
| | | | |

3   Explain how Lady Macbeth is affected by her conscience during the play after the murder of Duncan. Look carefully at her sleepwalking scene (Act 5 scene 1).

## *Extension*

Imagine that after Act 5 scene 1 Lady Macbeth seeks out her husband for a private conversation about how they feel about what they have done. Think about this and then choose either **1** or **2** below.

**Work with a partner**

1   Work out, rehearse and then perform the conversation they have.

**Work on your own**

2   Write out their conversation in the form of a play script.

# Justice

There is a sort of natural justice at work in the play and Macbeth is aware of this when he fears the 'judgement' he will eventually have to face for murdering Duncan. He realises that this terrible crime will 'return | To plague th' inventor' (Act 1 scene 7 lines 9–10). In other words, his crime will rebound on him. We might say that 'he who lives by the sword dies by the sword'. In effect, at the end of the play Macduff executes Macbeth for his crimes and the rightful heir to the throne, Malcolm, is crowned King.

Here are four traditional elements of natural justice:

- Some form of compensation for the victim
- Punishment for the criminal
- The triumph of right over wrong
- Freedom from oppression

**Work on your own**

1 Explain the extent to which the play makes use of these four elements.

2 How confident are you that justice will thrive in Scotland after Macbeth's death? Explain your thoughts.

# Nature and chaos

When Macduff first discovers Duncan's murdered body he announces: 'Confusion now hath made his masterpiece.' (Act 2 scene 3 line 64) He is horrified because he fears that the natural order of things has broken down and chaos will follow. The chaos that is triggered by the murder of a king is echoed in extraordinary events in the world of nature. For example, on the night of the murder Lennox reports that there was a terrible storm and

> ...*strange screams of death,*
> *And prophesying with accents terrible,*
> *Of dire combustion, and confused events...*
> (Act 2 scene 3 lines 54–6)

The next day, as the royal court tries to come to terms with the murder, Ross and an old man recall some unnatural events that happened in the lead-up to the murder: apparently a falcon was killed by an owl and Duncan's horses went wild, turned against their handlers and ate each other (Act 2 scene 4 lines 10–18).

**Work on your own**

1   Re-read Act 2 scene 4.

2   Explain at least four unnatural events that Ross and the Old Man discuss.

3   How does their choice of language (words) emphasise their feelings of horror about these events?

4   Use a table like the one below to explore the effect of their language. One example has been done for you.

| Example of their language | What they mean | How do these words emphasise their feelings of horror? |
|---|---|---|
| ...darkness does the face of earth entomb... (line 9) | Although it is day there is no light and so it seems like night time. | The choice of the word 'entomb' is a metaphor that directly connects the darkness to death and graveyards, and these are often associated with horror. |
|  |  |  |

5   The words 'nature', 'natural' and 'unnatural' appear a number of times in the play. Read the following references to nature/natural and unnatural and the speeches in which they appear:

*   'Against the use of nature?' (Act 1 scene 3 line 137)
*   'no compunctious visitings of nature' (Act 1 scene 5 line 45)
*   'Nature seems dead' (Act 2 scene 1 line 50)
*   'like a breach in nature' (Act 2 scene 3 line 111)
*   'The least a death to nature' (Act 3 scene 4 line 28)
*   'the natural ruby of your cheeks' (Act 3 scene 4 line 114)
*   'He wants [lacks] the natural touch' (Act 4 scene 2 line 9)
*   'Unnatural deeds | Do breed unnatural troubles' (Act 5 scene 1 lines 70–1)

**Work in a group of three to five**

1  Choose at least two of the references on the previous page and prepare a tableau to express each quotation. (See the section on drama and performance for more on tableaux.)

2  **a**  Draw a table with three columns. Head the columns 'Unnatural', 'Evidence', and 'Explanation'.

    **b**  Add detail to the table to examine ideas about what counts as 'unnatural' in the play.

    To help you do this, look up and explore the references listed. You could explore other parts of the play as well.

3  Prepare a presentation for the rest of the class in which you explain your ideas by referring to some of the text references.

# Gender roles

Modern audiences are often struck by how differently male and female characters are expected to behave in this play. In fact Lady Macbeth is aware of these different expectations and turns them to her advantage.

Firstly, as one of her methods of persuading Macbeth to kill Duncan, she accuses him of being unmanly: she tells him that when he first suggested murder 'then you were a man' (Act 1 scene 7 line 49) and by pursuing his ambitions he 'would I Be so much more the man' (Act 1 scene 7 lines 50–1).

Secondly, when Duncan's body is discovered, as a woman Lady Macbeth is beyond suspicion. Macduff automatically assumes that 'The repetition [of the news] in a woman's ear I Would murder as it fell' (Act 2 scene 3 lines 83–4). Macduff takes it for granted that Lady Macbeth is a 'gentle lady' (Act 2 scene 3 line 81). This assumption might seem naïve to us, but it should perhaps have seemed naïve even at the time. After all, the witches have considerable power and ruthlessness although they are clearly women – despite their beards!

In order to prepare herself to murder Duncan Lady Macbeth has already felt the need to 'unsex' herself in order to put aside her 'natural' womanly feelings and make herself 'top-full I Of direst cruelty' (Act 1 scene 5 lines 42–3). She is eventually driven into madness and – presumably – suicide by her guilt over the murders that she has been partly responsible for, so perhaps her attempt to lose her feminine gentleness is in the end unsuccessful.

However, being manly is not just about ruthlessness. When Macduff hears of the slaughter of his family we learn of other manly virtues.

### Work in a group of three

1 Read Act 4 scene 3 lines 204–40. Look carefully at what Macduff and Malcolm say about how Macduff should react to the terrible news.

2 What ideas about manliness are suggested in this section of the play?

3 Actors often find this part of the play difficult to perform convincingly. Why do you think that might be? What difficulties might the actors face?

4 Prepare this section of the play for a performance, each of you taking one of the parts. Here are some key questions for you to consider:

   a How will Ross deliver the news?

   b How will Macduff react to the news and to Malcolm's advice?

   c How will Malcolm insist on his version of manliness while being sympathetic to Macduff?

# Writing about *Macbeth*

When you write about the play – even in a test – you should go through six stages:

1   Read the question and make sense of it.

2   Develop your ideas.

3   Plan.

4   Write.

5   Edit your writing.

6   Check that your writing is accurate.

## Step 1: Read

The purpose of an assessment task is to give you the opportunity to discuss an aspect of the play in detail. In doing that you will show:

- your understanding of the play
- your appreciation of how it has been written and put together (language and structure)
- some idea of the play's relevance to its own time or ours.

---

**Macbeth kills Duncan only after a lot of thought and some detailed discussions with his wife.**

Why does Macbeth finally decide to kill Duncan?

---

The first thing to do is to identify the key words in the question. These are the words that show you exactly what the question is about. Here is the question again with the key words underlined:

<u>Why</u> does Macbeth finally decide to <u>kill Duncan</u>?

Now the point of the question becomes clear: it is about the reasons ('why') that led to Macbeth's decision to kill Duncan.

## Step 2: Develop

Even in a test it is better to spend a few minutes planning your writing rather than rushing straight into it. Before you can make a plan, you need to develop your ideas. Start by writing down the question's key words on a clean page:

Then jot down thoughts that might be relevant to those key words and the given scenes:

Now use arrows to mark possible links between your thoughts:

Add pieces of evidence (for example, short quotations) that you might be able to use in your writing to support your ideas, but also be prepared to cross out thoughts that don't seem to fit in very well:

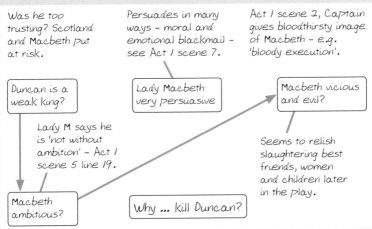

231

# Step 3: Plan

Now you need to shape your ideas into a plan. This provides the structure, or order, of your writing.

1 You need an introduction that explains:

   a what the task means for you

   b why this topic is an important one.

Think about the various reasons that might have led Macbeth to murder the king. However, don't answer the question yet; just get your reader interested! Here is an example of a lively and engaging opening:

> What makes a national hero turn into a vicious murderer? What makes a brave soldier who has risked his life in battle for his country turn against the king who has praised and honoured him, and slaughter him in cold blood? A fatal combination of factors led Macbeth down this path.

2 At the end of the answer you need a concluding paragraph. This sums up your most important points and answers the question directly.

3 Now for the tricky part: you need a series of paragraphs that bridge the gap between the introduction and the conclusion. Look back at the question and at the ideas you have come up with in your diagram. This will help you with the main points you need to cover before answering the question in your conclusion.

| Paragraph | Topic of paragraph | Focus |
|-----------|-------------------|-------|
| 1 | Introduction | Grab your reader's interest relevantly. |
| 2 | Influence of the witches. How they lead Macbeth 'astray'. | Act 1 scene 1, scene 3; Act 3 scene 5; Act 4 scene 1 |
| 3 | Influence of Lady Macbeth: how crucial was it? How does our view of her change due to later events? | Act 1 scene 4, scene 7; Act 5 scene 1 |
| 4 | Did Duncan 'deserve' to die? Was he a risk to Scotland? | Act 1: the war; his trust of Cawdor & Macbeths. |
| 5 | Macbeth's personality and ambitions | Act 1 scene 2 (battle reports); his reaction to witches' prophecy. |
| 6 | What more do we learn about Macbeth later in the play? | What Macbeth says and does after Act 2 scene 2. |
| 7 | Conclusion | Answer the question. |

# Step 4: Draft

Whatever the writing task, you need to explore most of these things:

- The play's ideas and meaning
- Its structure
- Its characters
- Audience (or reader) reaction
- Stagecraft: how the play is performed
- The language of the play

## *Point, Evidence, and Explanation*

It is easy to become vague when you are writing. Planning will help you to stick to the point and to organise your ideas so that you develop and explain them rather than keep repeating them.

PEE – point, evidence, and explanation – is a useful formula for expressing your ideas clearly. Here is an example relating to paragraph 4 of the essay:

---

When Duncan arrives at the Macbeths' home he instinctively feels he doesn't need to be on his guard [POINT]: he says the castle 'hath a pleasant seat' that 'sweetly recommends itself'. [EVIDENCE] This might simply reflect Duncan's warm sense of gratitude to Macbeth for saving Scotland in war. However, Duncan has already showed himself to be too trusting: the 'absolute trust' he put in the Thane of Cawdor almost led to military disaster. [EXPLANATION]

---

To explore ideas and evidence try to use words such as *could*, *might*, and *perhaps*. These help you explore more than one possibility – as in the example above.

# Step 5: Edit

When you have finished your first draft you should read through your work carefully to make sure it actually says what you mean. As you read it through, try to imagine that you are the person who will mark it. What would they think of what you have written? Ask yourself:

- Have I used Point, Evidence, and Explanation (PEE)?
- Have I explored ideas and considered alternatives?
- Are my sentences clear and to the point, or are they vague?
- Have I missed out anything crucial?
- Is everything relevant to the task?

Make any changes needed.

# Step 6: Check

When you are satisfied with your answer, make a final check for:

- grammar
- punctuation
- spelling.

# Writing tasks and questions

Each of the following varied writing tasks should allow you to show:

- your understanding of the play
- your appreciation of how it has been written and put together (language and structure)
- some idea of the play's relevance to its own time or ours.

After each of the first two tasks you will find some suggestions as to how you might meet each of the above requirements in your answer.

Look carefully at each task and work out what it is asking for. Start off by underlining the key words.

1   Choose three or four scenes in the play that contain images of darkness.  How might the darkness imagery in those scenes affect the mood of the play and the feelings of the audience?

    **Understanding**: how does the imagery provide a vehicle that develops the theme of evil?
    **Language**: explore examples of imagery and their likely effects.
    **Structure**: how does the darkness imagery provide a unifying thread running throughout the play?
    **Relevance**: how might a modern audience and an audience in Shakespeare's time be affected differently by this imagery?

2   **Act 1 scene 7 and Act 2 scene 2 lines 14–71**:
    What advice would you give to the actors in these two sections of the play to help them show the relationship between Macbeth and Lady Macbeth?

    **Understanding**: the sort of relationship you try to show must be justified by your understanding of the play.
    **Language**: examine how their choice of words gives clues about how they feel about each other.

**Structure**: suggest how the second section could build on how the first section was performed.

**Relevance**: how might a modern audience and an audience in Shakespeare's time expect different treatments of the relationship?

3 Choose a character from the play who could be considered a hero. Carefully explain with reference to the play text:

   **a** what makes your chosen character a hero

   **b** how the audience might feel about them

   **c** how an actor playing that character might emphasise their heroic aspects.

You are free to choose any character including:

| | | |
|---|---|---|
| Macbeth | Lady Macbeth | Macduff |
| Malcolm | Ross | Banquo |

4 **Act 2 scenes 3 and 4**:
How do these two scenes develop a theme of the battle between chaos and natural order? Refer closely to details in the text to support your ideas.

5 Some people have noticed similarities between the events in *Macbeth* and events in our own time.

Answer either:

   **a** What useful lessons might the play of *Macbeth* offer to people in the twenty-first century? Explain your ideas by referring closely to the text.

or:

   **b** How might a twenty-first century director of *Macbeth* draw attention to parallels between the play and our own world?

6 At the end of Act 5 scene 3 the doctor sounds desperate to get away from Macbeth's castle. Imagine that the doctor writes a detailed letter to a friend in England. In the letter he explains:

   • what has gone wrong with Scotland

   • what he has learned about Lady Macbeth

- what he has overheard from other characters
- how he feels about his country and Macbeth
- his fears and/or his hopes for the future.

Write the doctor's letter to his friend.

7 Look carefully at how the witches and the supernatural are presented in the play. Explain possible differences between how a modern and a Shakespearian audience might react to the witches and the supernatural.

8 Imagine you are going to put on a production of *Macbeth*. Explain how you would like the audience to react to the witches and how you will attempt to build those reactions. Refer in detail to Act 1 scene 3 and Act 4 scene 1 to explain your ideas.

In order to prepare for this task you should consider:

a whether the witches should be real, imaginary, symbolic, etc.

b the importance of the witches in the play

c the use of lighting, sound, costume, etc.

# Glossary

In these explanations, words that are in **bold** type are explained separately in the Glossary.

**alliteration**
a figure of speech in which a number of words close to each other in a piece of writing contain the same consonant sound: 'I am cabined, cribbed, confined' (Act 3 scene 4 line 23). The repeated 'c' sound draws attention to these words to strengthen their effect.

**apostrophe**
a figure of speech in which a character speaks directly to a person who is not present or to a **personification**. In Act 1 scene 5 Lady Macbeth says, 'Come you spirits...' (line 40). She may not be literally calling to spirits; she may just be trying to bolster her determination.

**aside**
a speech made by one of the characters for the ears of the audience alone, or purely for the benefit of another character on stage. For example, when Macbeth hears the witches' predictions in Act 1 he keeps confiding his thoughts to the audience while keeping them hidden from Banquo, Ross, and Angus. See also **soliloquy**.

**blank verse**
Shakespeare wrote his plays using a mixture of **prose** and verse. The lines of verse sometimes **rhymed** but more often did not rhyme. Verse that does not rhyme is called blank verse.

**caesura**
a pause or interruption in the middle of a line of verse (from the Latin word meaning 'to cut'). For example, when Macbeth is about to kill Duncan and is agonising over it, he suddenly stops his thoughts in the middle of a line, and returns his attention to the imaginary dagger: 'Or else worth all the rest. I see thee still' (Act 2 scene 1 line 45).

**contraction**  shortening a word or words by missing out some of the letters. The missing letters are shown by an apostrophe. Modern examples are *she's* (for *she is*) and *shan't* (for *shall not*). In Shakespeare's time other contractions were also used, such as *'tis* (for *it is*) and *show'st* (for *showest*).

**dramatic irony**  a situation in a play when the audience (and possibly some of the characters) knows something one or more of the characters do not. In a pantomime, for example, young children will often shout to tell the hero that a dreadful monster is creeping up behind him, unseen. For example in Act 1 scene 6, Duncan calls Macbeth's castle 'pleasant' and relaxes. However, we know that the Macbeths are already plotting his murder.

**end-on staging**  a form of staging in which the audience sit in rows all facing the same way with the stage at one end.

**enjambement**  sometimes in blank verse there is a natural pause at the end of a line. At other times there is no break and the sentence just runs over onto the next line. For example: 'And all our yesterdays have lighted fools | The way to dusty death' (Act 5 scene 5 lines 22–3). This running on is called enjambement (from the French word for 'span').

**exeunt**  a Latin word meaning 'They go away', used for the departure of characters from a scene.

**exit**  a Latin word meaning 'He (or she) goes away', used for the departure of a character from a scene.

239

**extended image**  most **images** are fairly short, taking up no more than a line or two. Sometimes a writer builds up an image so that it runs on for several lines. This is called an extended image. In Act 1 scene 7 Macbeth develops a comparison between his ambition and jumping over hurdles in a horse-race:
'I have no spur | To prick the sides of my intent, but only | Vaulting ambition, which o'erleaps itself, | And falls on th' other' (lines 25–8).

**figurative language**  language that is being used so that what is written or said is not literally true, usually for some kind of special effect. **Metaphors** and **similes** are examples of figurative language. For example, when Macbeth uses the metaphor that 'Life's but a walking shadow, a poor player' (Act 5 scene 5 line 24) he means it figuratively rather than literally.

**hyperbole**  deliberate exaggeration, for dramatic effect. For example, it is a dramatic exaggeration when Macbeth says that 'tears shall drown the wind' (Act 1 scene 7 line 25).

**iambic pentameter**  a line of **verse** which contains ten syllables, with a repeated pattern of weak and strong beats:
And **wash** this **fil**thy **wit**ness **from** your **hand**
ti **tum** ti **tum** ti **tum** ti **tum** ti **tum**
(Act 2 scene 2 line 45)
See also **metre**, **rhythm**.

**imagery**  **figurative language** in which the writer communicates an idea by creating a picture in the mind of the reader or listener. Types of figurative language include **metaphors** and **similes**.

**irony**

When someone says one thing and means another. Sometimes it is used to tease or satirise someone, or it can express great bitterness. For example, in Act 3 scene 6 lines 1–17, Lennox mocks Macbeth's version of events by pretending to agree with it.
See also **dramatic irony**.

**metaphor**

a figure of speech in which one person, or thing, or idea is described as if it were another. For example, in Act 1 scene 2, the Captain reports that when Macbeth killed Macdonald he 'unseamed him' (line 22). This metaphor is taken from tailoring. It suggests that Macbeth is cool, precise, and unemotional in battle.

**metre**

the regular pattern of weak and strong beats in a line of verse. The commonest metre in Shakespeare's plays is iambic. Each section consists of two syllables. The first is weak and the second is strong. See **iambic pentameter**.

**myth**

a traditional story, often very old. Myths often explain important events in the life of a people and they often refer to the lives of gods or other supernatural creatures.

**onomatopoeia**

using words that are chosen because they mimic the sound of what is being described.

**oxymoron**

**figurative language** in which the writer combines two ideas which are opposites. This frequently has a startling or unusual effect. For example, in Act 1 scene 1 the witches announce that 'Fair is foul, and foul is fair' (line 10).

**personification**

referring to a thing or an idea as if it were a person. For example, Macbeth says 'Thy very stones prate [tell] of my whereabout' (Act 2 scene 1 line 58). In suggesting that stones can talk, Macbeth is personifying them.

241

**play on words**    see **pun**.

**prose**    the form of language that is used for normal written communication. It is contrasted with **verse**.

**proverb**    a common saying that is used by many people. Proverbs usually express something that is useful knowledge, or that people think is useful. For example, 'Many hands make light work.' Shakespeare often uses proverbs in his plays, and many quotations from Shakespeare plays have become proverbs. This is true of Malcolm's comforting advice that 'The night is long that never finds the day' (Act 4 scene 3 line 240).

**pun**    a figure of speech in which the writer uses a word that has more than one meaning. Both meanings of the word are used to make a joke. An example is when in Act 1 scene 4 Duncan says: 'True worthy Banquo; he is full so valiant, | And in his commendations I am fed; | It is a banquet to me' (lines 54–6). Presumably Duncan is punning on the two words, 'Banquo' and 'banquet'.

**rhetorical question**    a question used for effect, usually in argument or debate, sometimes in a **soliloquy**. An answer is not expected; it would break the flow of the speech if it were offered. Lady Macbeth uses a string of rhetorical questions in Act 1 scene 7 lines 35–41 when she is trying to shame Macbeth into carrying out the plan to murder Duncan.

**rhyme**    when two lines of **verse** end with the same sound, they are said to rhyme. Shakespeare often makes use of rhyme, both in the middle of scenes and to round them off. For example, to finish Act 2 scene 4 the old man says to Ross: 'God's benison go with you, and with those | That would make good of bad, and friends of foes' (lines 40–1).

**rhythm**    the pattern of weak and strong syllables in a piece of writing. Shakespeare writes in **iambic pentameters,** but varies the way he uses them by breaking the rules. So his lines are mainly regular but with a lot of small variations. This combination makes up the rhythm of the verse. For example, look at how these two lines slightly depart from iambic rhythm: 'Take any shape but that, and my firm nerves | Shall never tremble. Or be alive again' (Act 3 scene 4 lines 101–2).

**satire**    making fun of something that you dislike or wish to criticise, by sending it up in some way. An example is Lennox's speech at the start of Act 3 scene 6.

**simile**    a comparison between two things which the writer makes clear by using words such as *like* or *as*. For example, when Macbeth is trying to decide whether to kill Duncan he describes pity as being 'like a naked new-born babe' (Act 1 scene 7 line 21).

**soliloquy**    when a character is alone on stage, or separated from the other characters in some way, and speaks either apparently to himself or herself, or directly to the audience. There are many examples of these in *Macbeth*, particularly early in the play when characters are mulling over secret thoughts and wrestling with their consciences. See for example Macbeth's soliloquy at the start of Act 1 scene 7. Soliloquies reveal characters' thoughts.

**theatre-in-the-round**    a form of theatre in which the audience sit all round the acting area.

**thrust stage**    a form of theatre in which the stage projects out into the audience, which thus sits on three sides of it. Shakespeare's Globe Theatre was like this, and so are the modern one in London, and the new Royal Shakespeare Theatre in Stratford-upon-Avon.

**verse**    writing that uses regular patterns, such as **metre** and **rhyme**.